US NAVY FIGHTERS

1960-1990

US NAVY FIGHTERS

1960 – 1990

Angelo Romano

Front cover The F-8 Crusader was one of the most stylish fighters ever to grace a carrier deck, and the colourful schemes which proliferated on these aircraft at the time further accentuated their aggressive lines. This 'subtle jet' belonged to VF-84 'Jolly Rogers', who at the time decided to go with decorative flames emanating from the Crusader's distinctive intake, rather than their now famous skull and crossbones on an all-black tail.The squadron discarded the flames in 1964 when they transitioned from the F-8C to the new generation F-4B Phantom II *(US Navy photo)*

Published in 1992 by Osprey Publishing Limited
59 Grosvenor Street, London W1X 9DA

© Angelo Romano

ISBN 1 85532 222 6

Written and edited by Tony Holmes
Page design by Paul Kime
Printed in Hong Kong

Back cover VF-143 'World Famous Pukin' Dogs' were one of the first Atlantic Fleet units to replace their F-4s with the F-14, the squadron actually conducting their transition training on the West Coast with the Fleet Replacement Squadron VF-124 'Gunfighters'. Once fully up to speed on the Tomcat, VF-143 (and sister-squadron VF-142 'Ghostriders') packed their bags and moved from Miramar to Oceana, Virginia, in 1976 *(Carlo Tripodi via Angelo Romano)*

Title page Along with the 'Felix and the bomb' emblem of VF-31 'Tomcatters', the boar's head of VF-11 'Red Rippers' is one of the oldest images associated with US naval aviation. The original badge first appeared on Curtiss biplane fighters assigned to VF-5B in the late 1920s, the boar's head adorning no less than 24 separate fighter aircraft types over the ensuing decades. When the design was originally copied directly from the Scottish Gordon family's coat of arms, little thought was given to any copyright infringement. In 1956 the then boss of the squadron, Cdr E L Feightner, wrote to the Gordon's Dry Gin Company requesting future use of the badge. He received the following letter in response;

'Dear Commander Feightner,
We received your letter of March 22nd and enclosures concerning the use of our Boar's Head trademark as part of the insignia of your fighter squadron 'Red Rippers'. We were, of course, delighted to hear that the fame of our Boar's Head mark attracted the attention of the United States Navy as early as 1927, and have no objection to your use of it as part of your squadron insignia. We would be most interested in receiving copies of the narrative history of the 'Red Rippers'. We admire your toast, but feel that the toast might be an empty boast unless the Gin is Gordon's. To assist you in this regard we shall send you shortly under separate cover 12 martini cocktail pitchers, but we must warn you that like Cinderella's stagecoach these pitchers will turn into pumpkins unless Gordon's Gin is used!
Yours Faithfully,
T L Elgard
Secretary
Gordon's Dry Gin Company Limited'
It is unlikely that the pitchers have survived the past 36 years, but the badge is still with VF-11. This suitably marked F-14A was photographed aboard USS *Forrestal* (CV-59) in February 1990 as Carrier Air Wing Six (CVW-6) cruised the Mediterranean during the carrier's penultimate operational deployment *(Angelo Romano)*

For a catalogue of all books published by Osprey Aerospace
please write to:

The Marketing Department, Octopus Illustrated Books,
1st Floor, Michelin House, 81 Fulham Road, London SW3 6RB

Acknowledgements

Special thanks go to the following people (alphabetically listed) and organizations who kindly helped the author during the compilation of this book; Jean-Charles Boreux; Lt Scott Campbell (PAO NAS Naples); RADM Pete Cressy (COMFAIRMED); Russel Egnor (CHINFO); Capt Bill Franson (Op-5); Lt Jim Fallin (COMSTHFLT assistant PAO); VADM Jack Fetterman (COMNAVAIRPAC); Lt Seamus Flatley; Harry Gann (Historian Douglas Aircraft); Mike Grove; Cdr Al Jacka (OIC NAS Naples); Cdr Allan Junker (Retired); Capt Lou Lalli (COMNAVAIRLANT Staff); Andy and Piero La Puca; Robert Lawson (former editor The Hook); Lois Lovisolo (Grumman History Center); Alfredo Maglione;Alfonso Mino; Cdr Skip Nelson (COMFAIRMED Staff); Lt Cdr Dave Parsons (VF-32); Cdr Zip Rausa (Retired) (editor Wings of Gold); VADM Jack K Ready (COMNAVAIRLANT); Sandy Russel (Naval Aviation News); Cdr Chuck Sammons (Retired) (ANA); Cdr Larry Stampe (Air Boss CVN-71); Carlo Tripodi; Chris Ziebold (McDonnel Douglas Company); Mike Weeks. The author would also like to thank the Association of Naval Aviation Inc at Suite 200, Leesburg Pike, Falls Church, Virginia, 22041, and the Tailhook Association, Box 40, Bonita, California 91908.

About the author

Angelo Romano was born in 1955 in Naples, Italy. He is a widely published freelance journalist, artist and photographer. In a professional capacity Angelo is a fully qualified aeronautical engineer and he currently works for Alenia (Aeritalia and Selenia), the major Italia Aerospace Company, as assistant manager of the Military Transport Aircraft Sales and Marketing Department. During the past 15 years, he has focused his research and writing efforts on the history of US Naval Aviation from 1957, building-up a very comprehensive file that includes thousands of colour slides and prints, squadron patches and histories, books and flight manuals. He has published over 100 articles in newspapers and aviation magazines about US Naval Aviation. After joining the Association of Naval Aviation Inc (ANA), the author, and some friends from the US Naval community in Naples, established, on 10 February 1990, the first overseas and international ANA squadron – the 'Med Centurions' – during an official ceremony aboard USS *Forrestal* (CV-59). Angelo Romano was nominated 'commanding officer' of the squadron, and as such was 'ordered' to promote both the membership and the goal of the ANA – to stimulate and support Naval Aviation, providing greater liaison and communication between the military, academic and business communities on issues of maritime aviation, taking into account the continuous changes taking place in the world today. Angelo lives in Naples with his wife Marisa and their two son Alberto and Federico.

Foreword

Which branch of the armed forces of the United States of America is called upon most often to serve as the initial vanguard of American policy and resolve when peace is threatened? It is the United States Navy. Highly mobile, flexible and capable of conducting completely autonomous operations, the Navy's Carrier Battle Group (CVBG) is routinely the National Command Authority's first choice to flex American muscle and act as a deterrent to terrorism or naked aggression.

Among the extensive capabilities of the CVBG is its ability to conduct anti-air warfare, suppress enemy air defences, perform aerial reconnaissance and project power ashore. Over the last 30 years, the fighter aircrews and aircraft embarked in our aircraft carriers have been called upon on many occasions to carry out these missions throughout the globe.

Having spent the last 28 years flying Navy fighters, both in the operational and research and development arenas, I was delighted by Angelo Romano's request for me to open his treaties on US Navy fighter squadrons since 1960. I have flown all of the aircraft he writes about, have participated in many of the events, and know and have had the fortune to serve with many of the outstanding Navy fighter pilots and RIOs who have written fighter history since 1960.

I am confident aviation historians will look upon the last 40 years of the 20th Century as the 'Golden Age of Carrier Aviation'. During this period jet fighter aircrews and aircraft forged the way for the evolution of the 'Super Carrier': the most versatile and potent multi-mission weapon system in the world.

The author traces modern Navy fighter lineage from the introduction of the first supersonic carrier-based aircraft, to the first engagements and victories over North Vietnam; from the introduction of the F-4 Phantom II, known to many as a fighter-bomber during the Vietnam War because of its truly multi-mission capability, to the founding in 1968 of 'TOPGUN', to counter the F-4 crews initial difficulties with Vietnamese MiGs. The training programme resulted in an impressive 12.5 : 1 kill ratio by the cessation of the fighting in January 1973.

The F-14 Tomcat's introduction to the Fleet in 1974 marked the first operational employment of variable geometry winged aircraft aboard carriers. Tomcat victories over Libyan aircraft in 1981 and 1989 demonstrated the superiority of American aircrews over Soviet trained pilots and Soviet manufactured aircraft.

In August 1990 US Navy fighter pilots and RIOs once again deployed in large numbers to the Red Sea and Arabian Gulf regions, in response to the naked aggression of Iraq. The superior skills and training of our fighter crews, and the super machines they fly, played a decisive factor in the overwhelming victory in *Desert Storm*. And although our aircraft were dressed in tactical paint schemes and carried radar guide air-to-air missiles, capable of destroying enemy aircraft far beyond visual range, in the final analysis it was the young dedicated maintenance technicians who kept our fighters flying and the crews who flew those fabulous machines who made the difference. As a famous fighter pilot once said, 'everything else is rubbish'.

Vice Admiral Jack K Ready, US Navy
Commander Naval Air Forces Atlantic
August 1991

Right A modern naval battle group is an awesome weapon of war, and one that has thankfully been put to the test only sparingly over the past 30 years. Flanked by a varied assortment of warships and support vessels,USS *Ranger* (CV-61) cruises through the Red Sea in late December 1990 – only a matter of weeks prior to its participation in Operation *Desert Storm*. Heading the 'armada' is the battleship USS *Missouri* (BB-63), whilst the vessel sailing in the carrier's wake is the nuclear-powered cruiser USS *Long Beach* (CGN-9) *(US Navy photo)*

Contents

The colourful 1960s

A thoroughbred in every way, the immortal Vought F-8 Crusader was the last in the long line of true single-seat US Navy fighters. Painted up in the familiar 'checkerboard' squares of VF-211 'Fighting Checkmates', this F8U-1 (F-8A) was photographed aboard USS *Lexington* (CVA-16) in June 1959 as the carrier cruised in the Pacific during a WestPac deployment. Ranged up alongside the Crusader is an anonymous FJ-3 Fury, armed up with both an old 'fat' style 500 lb bomb and a new 'slim' version of the same weapon. Immediately prior to this cruise, the 'Fighting Checkmates' had been redesignated VF-211 as part of the Navy's major re-organization which had been instigated the year before; up until 9 March 1959 the unit had been VF-24 'Fighting Renegades'! The shuffling of units had been approved by the Chief of Naval Operations on 10 March 1958, the sweeping changes creating uniform Carrier Air Groups, providing more permanent group assignments to ships, and permitting a reduction of assigned units and aircraft without reducing combat readiness. The new organization also provided for permanent Replacement Air Groups (RAG) to be established on each coast, which were responsible for the training of both maintenance personnel and naval aviators, as well as conducting special programmes to ease the introduction of new aircraft into fleet service. The re-organization also ushered in the new two-letter tail code marking for Air Group aircraft, replacing the previous single-letter identification system. Following its redesignation, VF-211 found itself attached to Carrier Air Group (CVG) 21 (later CVW-21), the squadron remaining under the control of this wing until 1975, when the 'Fighting Checkmates' traded in their F-8Js for F-14A Tomcats at Naval Air Station (NAS) Miramar *(US Navy photo)*

Fine Florida skies provide a fitting background for a spotless F8U-1 from the East Coast RAG, VF-174 'Hell Razors', based at NAS Cecil Field. Assigned the dual role of combat flight training for pilots destined for fleet squadrons and maintenance training for personnel in key enlisted ratings critical to frontline F-8 units, VF-174 received its first six Crusaders in November 1957. Prior to taking on the RAG role for the Atlantic Crusader community, the 'Hell Razors' had themselves been sailing the oceans of the world equipped with firstly the F9F-8 Cougar, then the FJ-3 Fury and finally the F9F-8 Panther. The unit's association with the Crusader lasted until 1 July 1966 when VF-174 was redesignated VA-174 and issued with the A-7A Corsair II, the 'Hell Razors' continuing to perform RAG duties for the fleet until the impending retirement of the A-7 saw the squadron disestablish on 30 June 1988 (*US Navy photo*)

There are no signs of low-viz greys in this nostalgic ramp shot taken at NAS El Centro, California, during the 1958 Naval Air Weapons Meet, a then annual event open to all Navy fighter squadrons. The elegant delta-winged Douglas F4D-1 Skyrays in the foreground hail from FAGU ('TA' tailcode), FAWTUPAC ('PA' tailcode) and VF-101 'Grim Reapers' ('AP' tailcodes), whilst the seemingly endless line of Furies (both FJ-3s and -3Ms) wear the markings of GMGRU-1, FAGU and VU-7. At the end of the ramp are two A-1 Skyraiders, a pair of USAF F-100 Super Sabres and a solitary B-26 Invader! As part of the redesignation programme, FAWTUPAC (Fleet All-Weather Unit Pacific) was redesignated VF(AW)-3 'Blue Nemesis' a month after this photo was taken. Assigned the unique all-weather air defence role, the squadron was permanently based ashore at NAS North Island, California, and was controlled by the Continental Air Defense Command, 27th NORAD Division. Equipped with 30 F4D-1s, the 'Blue Nemesis' also flew F3D-2T Skynights and SNB-5 Expeditors for training and liaison purposes, thus making VF(AW)-3 the largest frontline unit in the Navy. Nicknamed the 'ten minute killers', the Skyrays maintained a 24-hour alert status and were responsible for guarding the southwest approaches to the Continental USA. VF-101 fulfilled a similar commitment to NORAD under the aegis of the Air Force's 32nd Division on the East Coast, the 'Grim Reapers' flying out of NAS Cecil Field. The Skyrays were finally retired from frontline service on 4 March 1963 when VF(AW)-3 was disestablished (*McDonnell Douglas photo via Harry Gann*)

Surrounded by suitably coloured deck handlers and armourers, a McDonnell F3H-2 Demon of VF-213 'Black Lions' rides the waist elevator up to the flightdeck of the *Hancock* in 1962. This aircraft has a single AIM-7 Sidewinder attached to its inner port pylon, and a very early AIM-7 Sparrow II missile slung under its starboard wing. At the beginning of 1960, the active duty fighter community consisted of 33 units, including the shore-based VF(AW)-3 and four RAG squadrons. A quartet of fighter types were operational at that time: six squadrons operated the F4D-1 Skyray, ten each the F3H-2 Demon and the F8U Crusader, and three were about to phase out the less than successful F11F-1 Tiger. The various air groups on both coasts tended to include one dedicated day-fighter squadron, equipped with either the F3H Demon or more often the F8U Crusader, and a single night-mission capable unit, operating the F4D Skyray or the F4H Phantom II, within their ranks. VF-213's association with the Demon lasted only four years, the squadron receiving its first F3H-2s in January 1960 at NAS Moffet Field, California – the unit had flown F2H-3 Banshee and F4D-1 Skyray fighters prior to receiving the Demons. Exactly four years later, the F3H-2s were replaced by the definitive McDonnell carrier fighter, the F-4 Phantom II *(US Navy photo)*

VF-14 'Tophatters' are the oldest active squadron in the Navy, their lineage dating back to September 1919. The holders of many records and a unit steeped in tradition, VF-14 were also the longest frontline operators of the F3H Demon, the squadron trading in their portly F3D-2 Skynights for the lanky McDonnell fighter in March 1956. Based at NAS Cecil Field, the 'Tophatters' took part in three Atlantic cruises with the Demon as part of CVG-1, embarked aboard the USS *Franklin D Roosevelt* (CV-42). This appropriately marked jet was photographed in the Mediterranean during the 1960 cruise, its pilot firmly bracing himself in anticipation of the impending cat shot. The large leading-edge slats have been fully deployed and the stabilators angled upward in an effort to give the rather under-powered Demon more lift on launch. VF-14 retired their Demons in January 1964, receiving F-4Bs in their place (*US Navy photo*)

By the end of the 1960s, this sight had become commonplace across the globe; however, when this shot was taken by a McDonnell company photographer in May 1961, the F4H-1 Phantom II had still to attain its sea qualifications. Distinctively marked up in the codes and colours of VF-101 Det A, the early-production F4H-1 tops up its tanks courtesy of a VAH-9 'Hoot Owls' A3D-2 Skywarrior. This seemingly routine rendezvous between fighter and bomber/tanker was actually an aerial 'pitstop' for the Phantom II crew, who were in the process of setting a new record transcontinental time between Los Angeles and New York during the Bendix Trophy Race held on 24 May. Codenamed *Project Lana*, the crew set a time of 2 hours 47 minutes between the two coastal cities *(McDonnell Douglas photo)*

Although built side by side on the St Louis production line, and flown by squadrons tasked with the same operational objectives, these two F4H-1s were based thousands of miles apart on either coast of the USA. Wearing the familiar 'NJ' codes so long associated with the Pacific RAG community, F4H-1 BuNo 148258 belongs to VF-121 'Peacemakers', the Miramar-based unit being the first West Coast fighter squadron issued with the Phantom II in early 1961. Leading the two-ship formation is a VF-101 Det A Phantom II, this jet carrying a dummy AIM-7 Sparrow round in the forward missile trough. Although technically based at NAS Key West in Florida, the 'Grim Reapers' established Detachment A at NAS Oceana, Virginia, in June 1960 in anticipation of the first Phantom II arrivals. Once the basic training syllabus was running smoothly, and a handful of units had successfully transitioned from Skyrays and Demons to Phantoms IIs, Det A stood down in February 1963, VF-101 then conducting its entire training programme from Key West. By the early 1960s, in order to standardize the aircraft types deployed, and with the advent of the all-weather F4H-1, the Air Groups' sister fighter squadrons were at last issued with the same equipment. The disestablishment of the last Skyray unit (VF(AW)-3) on 4 March 1963, and the retirement of the Demon by VF-161 on 21 September 1964, marked the beginning of a new era for the fighter community as only two basic aircraft types (the recently redesignated F-8 Crusader and F-4 Phantom II) were now employed by 30 fleet and four RAG squadrons (*McDonnell Douglas photo*)

'Nam

Whilst the early 1960s saw the fighter community undergoing drastic changes as new types entered squadron service, across the globe in South-east Asia, the deteriorating political situation in Vietnam was causing the alarm bells to sound in Washington. To many Americans, the stand being made by South Vietnam against the communist North symbolized the struggle of the 'free world' against socialism, and as such warrented military advisers in-theatre fighting alongside South Vietnamese troops. The Gulf of Tonkin incident, which saw North Vietnamese Navy patrol boats attack the US Navy destroyer USS *Maddox* (DD-731), dragged the might of the American military machine into action. One of the first squadrons involoved in the rapidly escalating conflict was the F-8E Crusader-equipped VF-51 'Screaming Eagles', who were embarked aboard USS *Ticonderoga* (CVA-14) under the control of CVW-5. Charged with protecting RF-8A recce flights over the Plain of Jars in Laos, a six-aircraft detachment from VF-51 had cross-decked to USS *Constellation* (CV-64) expressly to perform this harrowing mission as the embarked F-4Bs from VF-142 and VF-143 were not yet authorized to fly over the small Asian country. Flying countless sorties with VFP-63 Det F Crusaders from August to November 1964, the VF-51 detachment proudly returned to *Ticonderoga* in early December without having lost a single jet. Four years and two bitter war cruises later, this heavily weathered 'Screaming Eagles' F-8H is secured to bow cat one aboard USS *Bon Homme Richard* (CVA-31) prior to yet another MiGCAP sortie in support of CVW-5's three A-4 Skyhawk units (the F-model being marshalled onto the waist cat belongs to VA-93 'Blue Blazers'). On the line for a total of 135 days between 21 February and 13 September 1968, VF-51 scored its only Crusader MiG kills during this cruise; two MiG-21s fell to AIM-9 Sidewinders on 26 June and 1 August. The squadron went on to claim four more MiG-17s during its eventful 1972 cruise equipped with the F-4B aboard the USS *Coral Sea* (CV-43) *(US Navy photo)*

Left With the bridle and bracing wires firmly attached to the Crusader's underbelly, a green-shirted catapult crewman signals the all clear to the 'shooter' and heads for safety seconds before launch. Armed with only a single Sidewinder on each of the fuselage pylons, this F-8E from VF-53 'Iron Angels' is about to commence a training sortie during a brief lull between operational missions. Sister-squadron to the 'Screaming Eagles' during all of VF-51's wartime Crusader cruises, VF-53 bagged only a solitary MiG-17 during its time with Task Force 77, and this particular F-8E ('Firefighter 203'/BuNo 150349) was the jet that claimed it. Leading a four-ship formation of 'Iron Angels' into North Vietnam in support of a CVW-5 air strike on 27 July 1968, Lt Cdr Guy Cane in 'Firefighter 203' met four MiG-17s head-on, the F-8 pilots then splitting into fighting pairs and reefing into the enemy jets once they had passed through the formation. After a brief turning fight, Lt Cdr Cane achieved a lock-on to one of the MiGs and fired off a single Sidewinder, which detonated near the jet's tailpipe, shredding its starboard wing. BuNo 150349 was later modified to F-8J specs, before eventually being lost during a war cuise with VF-211 aboard USS *Hancock* (CV-19) on 28 November 1969, when the aircraft suffered hydraulic failure and the pilot was forced to eject *(US Navy photo)*

Below The gold stars and the camouflaged flight suit denote that this jet, and its young pilot, hail from VF-162 'Hunters', one of the most famous Crusader units of the Vietnam conflict. The 'Hunters' downed two enemy fighters during their time on the line, both with the F-8E aboard USS *Oriskany* (CV-34). The first was claimed by the unit's legendary CO, Cdr Dick Bellinger, on 9 October 1966. Flying TarCAP (Target Combat Air Patrol) for an A-4 strike from the carrier USS *Intrepid* (CVS-11), the three 'Hunters' Crusaders were vectored towards the incoming MiG-21s by an E-1 Tracer. Bellinger chased a single jet down over the jungle, where he ripple fired two Sidewinders at the fleeing fighter, destroying it with one of the missiles *(US Navy photo)*

On four of the five war cruises undertaken by VF-162, the squadron was partnered by VF-111 'Sundowners'. The wooden decks of *Oriskany*, *Intrepid*, *Ticonderoga* and *Shangri-La* were home to the shark-mouthed Crusaders between May 1966 and December 1970, the squadron having received its baptism of fire during an earlier war cruise aboard the USS *Midway* (CV-41) in 1965 when it partnered the F-4B-equipped VF-21 'Freelancers'. Ironically, the only VF-111 Crusader MiG kill in was scored by Lt Tony Nargi of the squadron's Detachment 11, whilst embarked aboard the veteran carrier USS *Intrepid* (CVS-ll). Tasked with providing fighter cover for the carrier's small Air Wing 10 (CVW-10), Det 11 completed two cruises with *Intrepid*, Nargi's MiG-21 being downed during the second tour on 19 September 1968. Flying F-8C BuNo 146961 on a MiGCAP mission protecting an A-4 strike force, Nargi and his wingman, Lt(jg) Alex Rucker, were vectored onto two high flying MiG-21s, which climbed even higher once they had spotted the Crusaders. Nargi positioned himself behind the now looping fighter and

blew its tail off with a Sidewinder. This kill was the eighteenth and last MiG score for the Crusader. Although VF-111 Det 11 had only lost a single F-8 during its two cruises aboard *Intrepid*, the parent unit was not quite as fortunate. Three pilots were shot down and killed during the *Midway* cruise of 1965; three Crusaders were lost in action on the debut cruise with *Oriskany* in 1966, although two pilots were recovered and a third was made a POW; four F-8Cs were downed on the 1967 tour, two pilots being recovered and two being interned (a total of 11 Crusaders were lost by both squadrons during this bitter cruise, CVW-16 losing no less than 29 aircraft and 12 pilots killed or MIA in combat, and a further ten aircraft and eight aircrew in operational sorties); no aircraft were lost in combat during the 1969 *Ticonderoga* cruise, although a single jet crashed during operational flying; and, to finish on a high note in the Crusader, not a single F-8H was lost by VF-111 during the 1970 WestPac aboard *Shangri-La (US Navy photo)*

The most successful MiG-killing unit to fly the F-8 was VF-211 'Checkmates', an experienced pre-war Crusader squadron who had first received examples of Vought's famous fighter in late 1957. Responsible for the destruction of eight MiG-17s, the 'Checkmates' scored all of these kills during two eventful cruises equipped with the F-8E aboard the *Hancock* (10 November 1965 to 1 August 1966) and the *Bon Homme Richard* (26 January to 25 August 1966). Assigned to CVW-21 throughout the war, VF-211 completed no less than eight combat tours, all but one of them being aboard the *Hancock*. In this dramatic photograph the pilot receives the 'thumbs up'

from the catapult officer as the deckcrewman signals that the well-weathered F-8J is firmly secured by bridle and brace to *Hancock*'s waist cat four during operations in the South China Sea in 1972. The unique angled wing is firmly locked in the seven degrees up position, and the leading-edge slats have been fully deployed. The small bullet fairing ahead of the cockpit contains an AN/AAS-15 infrared scanner, this device giving the pilot more accurate firing solutions for his AIM-9 Sidewinders; a single live Delta model is mounted on the fuselage pylon *(US Navy photo)*

The family resemblance is clearly apparent in this classic fair weather tanking shot taken over the Pacific in July 1970. The buddy refueller is a VA-153 'Blue Tail Flies' A-7A Corsair II, and its customer is a veteran F-8J from VF-194 'Red Lightnings'. Both squadrons were attached to CVW-l9 at the time, and their 'home' during this cruise was the 'Big O' – the weary USS *Oriskany* (CVA-34). Although the veterans of eight combat cruises aboard three different carriers, VF-194 failed to score a MiG kill during the war, and like VA-153, was disestablished soon after the cessation of hostilities. Despite their lack of success against the North Vietnamese Air Force, the 'Red Lightnings' managed to set two records with the Crusader; firstly, their February 1958 cruise with the F8U-1 aboard the *Hancock* marked the aircraft's service debut on deployment; and secondly, VF-194 pilots experienced more ejections (31 in total) than any other frontline Crusader fighter unit (VFP-63 (photo-recce) finished top of the tally with 60, and VF-124 (RAG) came in second with 42)*(US Navy photo)*

Right With the Vietnam conflict now over for VF-194, a squadron F-8J sits quietly on the Miramar ramp in July 1973, the majority of the unit's pilots still being away on post-cruise leave. The 'Red Lightnings' last war cruise lasted nine months, the squadron spending 169 days on the line between 29 June 1972 and 5 March 1973. Following this mammoth deployment, the 'Red Lightnings' remained shore-based for over two years, VF-194, along with sister-squadron VF-191 'Satan's Kittens', not heading out on a WestPac again until 16 September 1975. Re-united with CVW-19 and the *Oriskany* once more the 'Red Lightnings'' cruise was the final F-8 carrier deployment for any Navy fighter squadron; CVW-19 and the *Oriskany* were also disestablished and decommissioned following this historic voyage
(Peter Mancus via Angelo Romano)

Above The first US Navy squadron to down a MiG in South-east Asia was VF-96 'Fighting Falcons', although that MiG was a Chinese Air Force fighter, not a Vietnamese one. Downed by Lt(jg) Terence Murphy and Ens Ron Fegan over Hainan Island on 9 April 1965 during a BarCAP (Barrier Combat Air Patrol), the MiG-17 was never officially confirmed. Minutes after the MiG was splashed at high altitude by an AIM-7 Sparrow, Murphy and Fegan themselves were hit and their F-4B downed. Both crewmen were killed, and to this day it has never been officially revealed what destroyed BuNo 151403. This photo was taken aboard the USS *Enterprise* (CVN-65) in May 1966 during VF-96's first cruise aboard the carrier with CVW-9. The squadron lost no aircraft in combat during 131 days on the line, although two crews were forced to eject from their F-4Bs in December 1965 during training sorties
(US Navy photo)

After four eventful combat tours with the *Enterprise*, CVW-9 embarked aboard the USS *America* (CV-66) in Norfolk, Virginia, in April 1970 for their next Task Force 77 deployment. As this photo shows, VF-96 had by this stage received the latest model Phantom II – the F-4J – and dramatically redesigned its tail markings as well. Due to the halt on bombing targets north of the 19th parallel, this cruise was a relatively quiet one compared to the previous torrid tours aboard the 'Big E'. The CVW-9/*America* partnership only lasted a single WestPac, VF-96 next deploying to the Gulf of Tonkin aboard USS *Constellation* (CV-64) in November 1971 for the legendary *Linebacker I* cruise. By the time the squadron returned to Miramar in July 1972, VF-96 had downed eight MiG fighters, the 'Fighting Falcons' topping the US Navy tally board with ten confirmed kills. The only naval aces of the conflict, pilot Lt Randy 'Duke' Cunningham and RIO Lt(jg) Willie 'Irish' Driscoll, were members of VF-96 during this historic WestPac deployment *(US Navy photo)*

Although a fighter by both design and designation, the F-4 Phantom II proved to be an excellent attack aircraft during the Vietnam War, all users of the 'Rhino' dropping tens of thousands of pounds of ordnance on targets both in North and South Vietnam, as well as Laos and Cambodia; many more F-4s were lost to anti-aircraft fire and SAMs during strike missions than to Vietnamese fighters. Bombed up ready for another strike, 'Showtime 601', flown by VF-96's CO, Cdr Robert Norman, is carefully positioned over one of *Enterprise*'s waist cats. A former test pilot at VX-4, Norman assumed command of VF-96 on 21 August 1965, leading the squadron on its second combat cruise the following month. On station for 131 days in total, this WestPac was a long, gruelling affair for CVW-9, the air wing losing 19 aircraft (16 in combat) and 18 aircrew either killed or interned. Whilst at sea VF-96 flew Task Force 77 patrols (BarCAP and ForceCAP), strike escort (TarCAP), recce escort, MiG hunting (MiGCAP), rescue sorties (ResCAP and SARCAP), flak suppression and straight strike missions. During its time on the line the squadron notched up some impressive bombing statistics; 1285 combat sorties for a total of 2506 hours airborne (ten per cent of the air wing's total), and 711 tons of ordnance dropped (eight per cent of CVW-9's total). This particular F-4B had already flown 56 sorties when it was photographed in April 1966 *(US Navy photo)*

Sitting in behind a beautiful RA-5C Vigilante from RVAH-6 'Fluers', the crew of 'Freelancer 110' wait their turn to launch from bow cat two aboard the USS *Ranger* (CV-61). By the time VF-21 arrived on-station with the *Ranger* in December 1967 it had already experienced war cruises aboard the *Midway* (1965) and the *Coral Sea* (1966/67). During their first WestPac, the 'Freelancers' had been credited with two MiG-17s on 17 June 1965, these victories being the first official kills of the war. Spotted over cat one alongside 'Freelancer 105' is an A-7A Corsair II of VA-147 'Argonauts', this squadron successfully debuting the pugnacious 'SLUF' during the *Ranger 's* 1967/68 Task Force 77 cruise (*US Navy photo*)

Looking more like a Marine than a naval aviator in his jungle fatigues, an experienced pilot from VF-21 climbs aboard his F-4B, having completed the pre-flight walk-around. Dangling from his hip is a standard issue Smith and Wesson .38 service revolver, whilst atop the intake is a very stylish 'bone dome', suitably decorated in squadron colours. Although this cruise was the first of five consecutive WestPac sailings undertaken by VF-21 aboard the *Ranger*, it was the last operational deployment carried out by the squadron in the F-4B, the 'Freelancers' transitioning onto the Juliet model at Miramar in 1968. During the squadron's 88 days on the line between 3 December 1967 and 9 May 1968 two VF-21 F-4Bs were lost; BuNo 151492 'NE 101' on 16 December to AAA; and this jet, BuNo 153014 'NE 103' on 28 April 1968, also to AAA. All four crewmen were recovered after successfully ejecting from their stricken aircraft *(US Navy photo)*

Right The pilot keeps his eyes firmly fixed on the gesticulating catapult crewman as he is guided slowly over the launch shuttle. Surrounding the jet are a clutch of red-shirted armourers, ready to give the live AIM-9Ds a quick once over before the F-4B is shot off the deck, and several green-shirted aircraft handlers. One of over a dozen Phantom IIs assigned to VF-161 'Chargers', this aircraft was embarked aboard the *Coral Sea* at Alameda, California, in July 1967, prior to the carrier's nine-month long WestPac cruise. Although the 'Chargers' were successful MiG killers on two other cruises, the first *Coral Sea* deployment was not a happy affair for either VF-161, or its sister-squadron VF-151 'Vigilantes' – the 'Chargers' lost three F-4Bs (two in combat) and three aircrew killed, whilst the 'Vigilantes' lost no less than five Phantom IIs in combat, two of which were shot down by MiG-17s near Haiphong. All ten VF-151 crewmen were made POWs, with one later dying in captivity (*US Navy photo*)

Above Optimized for an anti-MiG mission, these F-4Bs from VF-161 are fully missiled up, with four AIM-7E Sparrow rounds nestling in the underfuselage troughs and four AIM-9D Sidewinders split between the two wing pylons. The standard McDonnell 600 gallon centreline tank was usually carried on every combat sortie, and although it had a high G rating, when it came to 'turning and burning' with an agile MiG-17 the pilot would invariably punch the external store off prior to engaging the enemy. Having completed another uneventful BarCAP over the *Constellation*'s battlegroup, 'Rock River 202' and '214' rendezvous with a KA-3B tanker from VAH-8 'Fireballers' for a JP4 exchange, before descending back into the recovery pattern. This cruise was VAH-8's first and only deployment with the 'Chargers' and CVW-15. The highlight of the VF-161's 111 days on line was the MiG-17 kill claimed by Lt William 'Squeaky' McGuigan and Lt(jg) Robert Fowler on the morning of 13 July 1966 whilst flying a TarCAP in F-4B BuNo 151500. Another six years would pass before VF-161 added to this solitary score (*US Navy photo*)

Some Pacific Fleet fighter squadrons like VF-92 'Silver Kings' and VF-213 'Black Lions' spent many months on the line protecting strike units throughout the nine years of the Vietnam conflict and only managed to down a single enemy aircraft (the 'Black Lions' destroyed an Antonov An-2 with an AIM-7E on 20 December 1966 and VF-92 claimed a MiG-21F on 10 May 1972). VF-31 'Tomcatters', and sister-squadron VF-103 'Sluggers', on the other hand, spent only 173 days with Task Force 77 on the line aboard USS *Saratoga* (CV-60) in 1972/73 and each claimed a MiG-21! The honour of scoring VF-31's only kill

of the war fell, rather appropriately, to the squadron boss, Cdr Samual C Flynn Jnr and his RIO, Lt William H John, on 21 June 1972. Flying his own personal jet (F-4J BuNo 157293), Flynn downed a MiG-21 with a Sidewinder during a MiGCAP sortie in support of a *Linebacker I* strike on Haiphong harbour. Signalled clear for launch, the crew of this F-4J brace themselves for the cat shot. Devoid of external stores, this Phantom II was photographed launching on a training sortie during a brief period off-station in the South China Sea in late August 1972 *(US Navy photo)*

The Vietnam conflict was fought in the main by West Coast squadrons embarked aboard carriers assigned to the Pacific Fleet. Miramar-based fighter units like VF-96 and VF-111 built up a vast wealth of combat experience as they regularly conducted WestPac cruises out to the Gulf of Tonkin on a six-monthly rotational basis. By the end of the war, most AirPac squadrons had completed between six and eight combat tours, and performed both fighter and strike missions. However, on the East Coast the Atlantic fighter community at Oceana had been used very sparingly over Vietnam, only VF-74 'Be-Devilers' experiencing two WestPac deployments, the first of which was cut drastically short by a disastrous blaze aboard the *Forrestal* on 29 July 1967. Similarly, AirLant's carriers were also under utilized, *America* topping the cruising table with three WestPac deployments. On the first of these tours, the carrier embarked CVW-6, and its nine squadrons, for the wing's one and only combat cruise, replacing the badly damaged *Forrestal* on station in the Gulf of Tonkin. On the line for 112 days between 31 May and 29 October 1968, the carrier was involved in some of the heaviest fighting of the war in support of *Rolling Thunder VI*. VF-33 'Tarsiers' and VF-102 'Diamondbacks' provided fighter cover for the strike units of CVW-6, both squadrons being equipped with the brand new F-4J; the Juliet model had not seen combat up to this point. Five Phantom IIs (three from VF-33 and two from VF-102) were shot down during the cruise; three fell to AAA, one to a SAM and VF-102's boss, Cdr W E Wilber, was lost in a dogfight with a MiG-17. The other 'Diamondbacks' jet lost was F-4B BuNo 155540 'AE 112', seen here spotted behind the F-4J that has just successfully trapped back aboard *America*. Hit by AAA during a strike mission on 25 July 1968, the aircraft's pilot, Lt C C Parish went down with the stricken jet, whilst his RIO, Lt R S Fant, ejected and became a POW *(US Navy photo)*

Now based at Oceana, VF-143 'Pukin' Dogs' were home-ported at Miramar during the Vietnam conflict. Veterans of seven combat cruises all with CVW-14, VF-143 were involved with Task Force 77 operations from the time of the first skirmishes in the Gulf of Tonkin in August 1964 right through to the final US withdrawl in mid-1973. Although spending many thousands of hours in combat, the squadron was only credited with a single kill – a MiG-21 was downed with an AIM-7E by Lt(jg) Robert P Hickey Jnr and Lt(jg) Jerry G Norris on 26 October 1967 during a MiGCAP sortie in F-4B BuNo 149411. Five F-4Bs were lost during this same cruise aboard *Constellation*, although only one of these jets belonged to VF-143 (the remaining four were VF-142 'Ghostriders' aircraft).

Four of the seven cruises undertaken by the 'Pukin' Dogs' saw the squadron embarked aboard the *Constellation*, the other three being shared with the *Ranger* (1965/66) and the *Enterprise* (1971/72 and 1972/73). Taking advantage of a break from flying stations, the bronzed sailors of VF-143's maintenance section give F-4B BuNo 151513 a thorough scrub down on the stern of 'Connie' in June 1967. The Battle Efficiency 'E' and the title 'BEST IN THE WEST' refer to the prestigious awards bestowed upon the squadron during their work-up period back at Miramar in early 1967, the 'Pukin Dogs' finishing top in the air combat and bomb delivery competitions held at the air station prior to the WestPac *(US Navy photo)*

One of only two squadrons to down a MiG in both the F-8 Crusader and the F-4 Phantom II, VF-111 was heavily involved in the conflict virtually from day one through to the cessation of hostilities. The 'Sundowners'' sole Crusader kill was achieved by Lt Tony Nargi and is detailed earlier in this chapter. Its solitary Phantom II victory was claimed by Lt Garry 'Greyhound' Weigand and Lt(jg) William 'Farkle' Freckelton in F-4B BuNo 153019 during a ForceCAP sortie on 6 March 1972. A single AIM-9D was used by Weigand to destroy the MiG-17 at a height of less than 500 feet as the *Fresco* attempted to shoot down another VF-111 F-4B that was

'bugging out' following an inconclusive dogfight with the Vietnamese fighter. Photographed during that very same cruise, 'Sundowner 203' is attached to bow cat two aboard the *Coral Sea* prior to launching on a strike mission in support of *Linebacker I*. Mounted on the combined missile/bomb pylons under the wings are four AIM-9D Sidewinders and 12 500 lb Mk 82 'slicks'. One more war cruise remained for VF-111 following the eventful 1971/72 WestPac, the final deployment aboard *Coral Sea* in 1973 being a relatively quiet affair compared to the year before *(US Navy photo)*

Post-war F-4s

Right Post-war, the Navy's sailing schedules for their carriers returned to the familiar pattern set during the more peaceful days of the 1950s and early 1960s – six-month cruises to either WestPac or the Indian Ocean for the Pacific Fleet, and the traditional Mediterranean deployment for Atlantic Fleet vessels. One squadron used to this routine was VF-11 'Red Rippers', the 'wild boars' of NAS Oceana maintaining a virtually unbroken record of deployments 'across the pond' from 1960 onwards. Invariably found aboard the *Forrestal* with CVW-17, VF-11 completed a series of Med cruises equipped with various models of the Crusader and the Phantom II, before eventually transitioning to the F-14 Tomcat in 1980. Photographed during the squadron's penultimate Atlantic cruise with the F-4J in May 1978, this pristine Phantom II served as the Commander Air Group (CAG) jet for VF-11 during the seven-month long deployment. Compared to some of the other 'CAG birds' knocking around in the fighter community at the time, BuNo 157283 was one of the more subdued examples of the breed. The CAG's RIO in this jet was obviously quite a colourful character judging by his name! (*Angelo Romano*)

Below Prior to receiving the F-4J in late 1973, the 'Red Rippers' accumulated a wealth of Phantom II experienced during an eight-year association with the Bravo model 'Rhino'. Swinging in behind a KA-3B tanker of VAH-10 'Vikings', this F-4B has just returned from a strike training sortie over one of the many bombing and rocket ranges on the island of Sardinia. Mounted on the starboard wing pylon is an empty LAU-3A rocket pod, whilst on the port hardpoint is an empty practice bomb ejector rack (*US Navy photo*)

Right Heading back for the carrier with both bomb racks empty, this F-4B was photographed skimming through the clouds on the same Med cruise as the previous 'Red Ripper'. *Forrestal* and VF-11 went to war over Vietnam in July 1967, although the squadron's taste of combat was to last only five days (between the 25th and 29th of that month) as a disastrous fire, caused by a rogue Zuni rocket being accidently shot off an F-4 into the bombed and fuelled up aircraft ranged ahead of it, virtually destroyed VF-11. The blaze raged for 17 hours and 134 lives were lost, as well as 21 aircraft (seven F-4Bs, eleven A-4Es and three RA-5Cs), whilst the carrier itself sustained $72 million worth of damage. A year after the fire, VF-11 and the *Forrestal* joined forces once again and headed east from Norfolk for a confidence boosting 6th Fleet cruise, the squadron completing three more tours between December 1969 and July 1973, before transitioning to the F-4J. Unlike most other Phantom II units, VF-11 painted the distinctive bulbous radome of their aircraft gloss white, maintaining a tradition first started with the Crusader in the early 1960s *(US Navy photo)*

Below The 'Red Rippers' have always been proud of their professionalism as a fighting unit, and in the heyday of colourful squadron markings in the 1970s, a fair amount of this pride was generated by the overall condition of the jets they flew. Positively radiating on the deck of *Forrestal* during an R and R portcall to Naples in August 1975, this beautiful F-4J belonged to the then XO of VF-11. Taking advantage of the fine weather, and the lack of flying, the squadron's technicians have extracted the aircraft's Westinghouse AN/AWG-59 radar from the slender nose of BuNo 157295. For some unexplained reason this jet wears a second squadron 'coat of arms' on its splitter vane, although this marking lacks the traditional lightning bolt between the 'meatballs'*(Angelo Romano)*

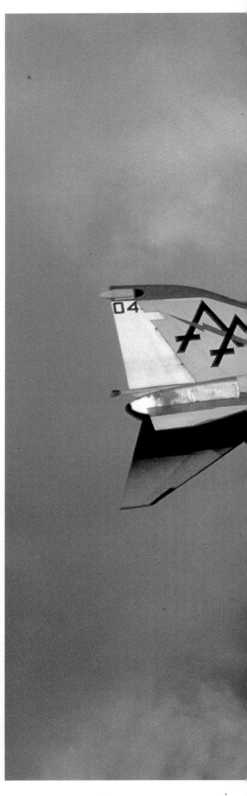

No less than 28 units flew the F-4 in squadron strength with the Navy between 1961 and 1986, and VF-21 'Freelancers' was one of a select group to fly all four major service variants. The squadron first operated the B-model in mid-1963, trading in their obsolete F3H Demons for brand new McDonnell fighters at Miramar. As recounted in the Vietnam chapter, VF-21 successfully completed three WestPac cruises with the Bravo model during the hardest years of the conflict before transitioning to the F-4J in 1968. The squadron endured another four Task Force 77 patrols, before embarking on a series of more peaceful WestPacs in the mid to late 1970s with CVW-2 aboard their wartime home, USS *Ranger*

(CV-61). During the last of these cruises with the F-4J, several of the squadron's jets spent some time based at NAF Atsugi, near Tokyo, whilst the *Ranger* operated in Japanese coastal waters. Crossing the runway threshold on finals to the base, the 'CAG-bird' of VF-21 shows the distinctive markings worn by the squadron's Phantom IIs during this final deployment in 1979. The aircraft wears gloss gull grey overall, and is devoid of the traditional CAG rainbow stripes. Just as VF-11 made the white radome their individual trademark, so the stylized black 'proboscis' became synonymous with VF-21's jets as well *(Masumi Wada)*

By 1981, VF-21 was operating a fleet of F-4Ns which were older than their recently traded in F-4Js! In between retiring the Juliets and re-equipping with the November models, the 'Freelancers' had flirted briefly with the ultimate Navy Phantom II, the F-4S. Having completed the transition from the J- to the S-model, the squadron commenced the extensive programme of pre-cruise work-ups prior to an eventual WestPac deployment aboard their 'new' home, the venerable *Coral Sea*. However, in late 1980 AirPac decided that the S-model's over-ramp recovery speed was too high for the small *Midway* class carrier, and VF-21, along with sister-squadron VF-154 'Black Knights', hurriedly swapped jets with the reserve units at Miramar, the 'Freelancers' receiving weary F-4Ns in place of their 'cooking' S-models. Now wearing Air Wing 14's 'NK' tail codes in place of CVW-2's 'NE', VF-21 eventually went to sea again in the summer of 1981. This Vietnam veteran was photographed at NAS Fallon, Nevada, during air wing work-ups in May 1981, just prior to the WestPac deployment *(Michael Grove)*

Above Arguably as famous as the Gordon's Gin emblem of VF-11, the 'Felix and the bomb' motif has adorned Navy fighter and attack aircraft since 1921 when the first black cat appeared on Combat Squadron Four's machines. Worn by VF-2, VF-6 twice (1927 and 1943), VB-2 and VF-3, 'Felix' and VF-31 were finally united in August 1948 when the F8F Bearcat-equipped VF-3A was redesignated at NAS Quonset Point, Rhode Island. Since then, VF-31 have carried the emblem on the F9F-2 Panther, F2H-2/3 Banshee, F3H-2 Demon and, of course, the definitive McDonnell Douglas Navy fighter, the F-4 Phantom II. Initially equipped with the Bravo model, the squadron received F-4Js in 1968; the legendary Phantom IIs were eventually replaced by F-14s in August 1980. Photographed four years prior to VF-31's re-equipment during a brief spot of R and R in Naples, this beauty (BuNo 153809) wears an appropriately marked centreline tank in celebration of the American Bicentennial (*Angelo Romano*)

Right A little younger than its elderly squadron mate featured in the last photo, BuNo l55562 is rigged up to 'Super Sara's' waist cat four during the 1977 Med cruise. Wearing full VF-31 colours, 'Tomcatter 101' is the personal mount of the squadron boss, although, as is normal Navy practice, any of the unit's crews would fly the jet if it was serviceable. A quick glance at the sailors' surcoats reveals a mixture of deck crew from both of CVW-3's fighter squadrons (*Angelo Romano*)

Returning from an intra-squadron ACM sortie out over the choppy Med, the crew of 'Tomcatter 112' vent full in an effort to reduce the aircraft's landing weight before trapping back aboard the *Saratoga*. The massive tailhook has already been extended beneath the jetpipes, and soon the F-4 will pass over the carrier before breaking left and entering the recovery pattern *(via Angelo Romano)*

Back in Naples harbour yet again for the annual *Saratoga* portcall during the carrier's 6th Fleet deployment, VF-31's maintenance crew have placed elderly F-4J BuNo 153891 up on jacks in order to rectify a minor technical glitch with the aircraft's undercarriage. Photographed in December 1977 during VF-31's penultimate Med cruise with the Phantom II, this aircraft wears a single shade of grey overall. By the late 1970s most squadrons still flying the Phantom II had removed the gloss white paint from the undersides of their jets, although, as can be seen in this photograph, few units toned down the traditionally flamboyant squadron markings. VF-31's only concession to the new low-viz era was the removal of the yellow disc which surrounded the 'Felix' emblem *(Angelo Romano)*

The distinctive 'Gold Star' marking on the tail of this weary F-4J clearly denotes that the jet belongs to VF-33 'Starfighters', an old and distinguished fighter unit that has been based at NAS Oceana since July 1954. Along with sister-squadron VF-102 'Diamondbacks', the 'Starfighters' (or 'Tarsiers' as they were formally known up until the mid-1980s) flew the Juliet model Phantom II longer than any other frontline unit. VF-33 received its first jets fresh from St Louis in early 1968, just prior to its one and only Vietnam cruise (aboard *America*). Achieving MiG killer status during this WestPac (a single MiG-21 was downed with a Sidewinder by Lt Roy Cash Jnr and Lt Joseph Kain Jnr on 10 July 1968), VF-33 returned to 6th Fleet operations in 1969, completing six deployments with CVW-7 aboard USS *Independence* (CV-62), before returning to CVW-6 in 1978 (the squadron had previously spent 15 years with this air wing between 1953 and 1968) and embarking on another two Med cruises. Photographed in August 1977 launching from one of 'Indy's' waist cats during its last CVW-7 cruise, this F-4J wears typical VF-33 markings of the period. The squadron hardly altered the appearance of its jets in the 1970s, the 'Starfighters' only losing their black tails and gold stars just prior to their final F-4J cruise aboard *Independence* in September 1980 (*Angelo Romano*)

Surrounded by the usual deck clutter found aboard a modern aircraft carrier, a 'Black Aces' F-4N sits chained down alongside USS *Franklin D Roosevelt 's* (CV-42) island during the vessel's penultimate Med cruise in 1975. VF-41's association with the Phantom II was a long and varied one, the unit being one of the first Atlantic Fleet fighter squadrons to receive the F4H-1, as it was then designated, in February 1962. An early task thrust upon the 'Black Aces' was a move to Key West to bolster North American Air Defense Command during the Cuban missile crisis. A handful of 6th Fleet deployments, and a single WestPac to Vietnam in 1965, filled VF-41's decade; all of these sailings were with CVW-7 aboard the *Independence*. In 1967 the squadron traded in their Bravo models for new F-4Js, the first Med cruise with the type being made in 1968/69. A change of air wings and a 'new' carrier greeted VF-41 in 1970, CVW-6 and the *Roosevelt* now playing host to the 'Black Aces'. After three routine 6th Fleet deployments, the squadron was then ordered to swap its F-4Js for F-4Bs and increase its aircraft strength from 12 to 18 jets in anticipation of an experimental Med cruise. The 1973 deployment was indeed a quite radical tour, VF-41's 18 weary Phantom IIs being the **only** fighter echelon embarked on the *Roosevelt*. During the cruise the 'Black Aces' spent a considerable period of time on a heightened alert status as the carrier monitored the Yom Kippur War from international waters off the coast of Israel. Back at Oceana in 1974, the squadron transitioned yet again, receiving a dozen F-4Ns in place of its 18 F-4Bs. Sharing the fighter duties once again with long-time sister-squadron VF-84 'Jolly Rogers', VF-41 returned to the Med for its final Phantom II deployment. Suitably adorned with VF-41's famous 'Ace of Spades' emblem, this F-4N (BuNo 151406) was assigned to the squadron's executive officer (XO), Cdr Scotty Scott, during the 1975 cruise; the 'Black Aces' unique ranking stripes on the cockpit coaming were a distinguishing feature of VF-41's jets at the time *(Angelo Romano)*

Only Reserve fighter squadrons were originally scheduled to receive the F-4N; VF-201 and -202 at NAS Dallas, Texas, and VF-301 and -302 at Miramar, were all due to replace their obsolete F-8J Crusaders with the reworked F-4Bs by 1975. However, delays in F-14 Tomcat procurement, allied with landing speed restrictions aboard the smaller *Midway*-class carriers, saw six frontline squadrons equipped with November model Phantom IIs for varying periods of times. One of these units was VF-51 'Screaming Eagles', a veteran multi-MiG killing squadron with no less than eight WestPac combat cruises to its credit. Among the last Crusader squadrons to transition onto the Phantom II, VF-51 only received its first F-4Bs in the spring of 1971. Despite its relative inexperience with the type, VF-51 still managed to down four MiG-17s during its first WestPac with the F-4 in 1971/72 aboard the *Coral Sea* – these kills added to the two MiG-21s

destroyed by the 'Screaming Eagles' in 1968 whilst the unit was equipped with the F-8H aboard USS *Bon Homme Richard* (CVA-31). Following a final Task Force 77 WestPac with the F-4B in 1973, the squadron returned to Miramar for re-equipment with the F-4N in early 1974. Photographed during work-ups with the 'new' Phantom II in April 1974, these suitably marked F-4Ns all wear newly applied squadron colours on their slab fins. The overall decoration of VF-51's F-4Ns mirrored the scheme adopted for the squadron's Bravo models following the unit's return to Miramar after their first WestPac with the Phantom II. Prior to that, VF-51 had liberally daubed the fuselage of their aircraft with the now famous 'supersonic can opener' motif; this stylized eagle was deemed a little too loud by CINCPAC and the squadron was ordered to tone down their F-4Bs accordingly! *(US Navy photos)*

The first operational squadron equipped with the Phantom II was VF-74 'Be-Devilers', the unit receiving its first F4H-1s in July 1961. Working closely with VF-101 (the Atlantic Fleet RAG), the squadron, under the leadership of Cdr Julian Shake, virtually wrote the operational manual for the F-4B over the next 12 months, VF-74 first taking the aircraft to sea aboard the *Saratoga* in October 1961. Fifteen years later, and now equipped with the F-4J, VF-74 was chosen to temporarily join CVW-8 for the wing's embarkation aboard the then brand new nuclear carrier USS *Nimitz* (CVN-68). Photographed near the vessel's island in November 1976 as the ship sailed through the Med, 'Be-Deviler 202' wears bicentennial stripes on its rudder and a single MiG kill star on the splitter plate. BuNo 153899 was never credited with a MiG kill; its pilot, squadron XO Cdr Robert 'Gene' Tucker Jnr, was however. Four years before this photo was taken, Tucker Jnr had been assigned to VF-103 'Sluggers' as a lieutenant commander, and had embarked with the rest of the unit aboard *Saratoga* in April 1972 for both the squadron's and the carrier's only combat cruise of the war. On the line for 173 days between 11 May 1972 and 8 January 1973, VF-103's kill was scored early on in the deployment. Flying F-4J BuNo 157299 on a MiGCAP sortie on 10 August 1972, Lt Cdr Tucker Jnr, and his RIO, Lt(jg) Stanley 'Bruce' Edens, locked up a MiG-21 at medium range and downed the fighter with a single AIM-7E Sparrow missile (*Angelo Romano*)

Between 1969 and 1977, VF-102 completed 11 6th Fleet deployments, the squadron's only break from this rather monotonous routine of Med cruises being a single WestPac aboard the *America* in 1968 in support of Task Force 77. During the squadron's 112 days on the line between 31 May and 29 October, the 'Diamondbacks' flew hundreds of strike missions with fellow Phantom II operators VF-33 – these two squadrons actually blooded the new F-4J in combat during the cruise. Unfortunately, four Phantom IIs were lost (two per squadron) and three crews killed in combat; VF-102's CO, Cdr W E Wilber, was actually shot down by a missile fired from a MiG-21 on 16 June 1968. Only five Navy F-4s were shot down by the NVAF during the whole conflict. Although Cdr Wilber safely ejected, his RIO, Lt(jg) B F Rupinski, was killed in the missile strike. Following the WestPac, VF-102 moved air wings to CVW-7 in March 1969, this switch also resulting in a change of carriers for the unit. Now calling the 'Indy' home, VF-102 completed six cruises with the carrier between June 1970 and October 1977, these immaculate jets being photographed over the Med during the last of these deployments. Briefly despatched to the Caribbean in 1978 as part of a composite air wing put together for the shakedown cruise of the recently commissioned USS *Dwight D Eisenhower* (CVN-69), VF-102 was transferred upon completion of this tasking back to CVW-6 (its very first Phantom II controlling wing), and the *Independence*. Two more 6th Fleet cruises were to follow between June 1979 and June 1981, before the squadron finally traded in its weary F-4Js (which it had operated continuously since late 1967) for new F-14s *(both via Angelo Romano)*

Above In 1974 four frontline units traded either up or down to the 'new' F-4N model Phantom II; one of those squadrons in the latter category was VF-111 'Sundowners'. Re-equipped with the F-4B in early 1971, VF-111 completed two war tours with the Bravo model aboard the *Coral Sea* before converting to the F-4N at Miramar in December 1974. The November model Phantom II was basically an updated F-4B, 178 Bravos built between serial blocks 12 and 28 being chosen for overhaul at the Naval Air Rework Facility (NARF) at North Island as part of Operation BEE-LINE. The F-4s picked for refurbishment were broken down to components, re-stressed and thoroughly fatigued tested. Old, worn parts were replaced with new, more efficient ones, resulting in an extended service life into the 1980s. The helmet mounted Visual Target Acquisition System (VTAS) was fitted into the cockpit, as well as a dog-fighting computer, air-to-air IFF (Identification Friend or Foe), one-way data link and an auto altitude reporting system. The aircraft's short-range ACM capability was also improved with the fitment of the Sidewinder Expanded Acquisition Mode (SEAM) to the F-4's fire-control radar. For self-protection, Sanders AN/ALQ-127

ECM antennae were scabbed onto both intake fairings, whilst other smaller excrescences associated with the AN/ALQ-126 RHAW system appeared beneath the wings and atop the fin. The first reworked F-4N flew at North Island on 4 June 1972, with refurbished airframes entering fleet service the following February. This suitably marked Phantom II was photographed at NAS Fallon during May 1976, four months prior to completing a single Med cruise with CVW-l9 and the *Roosevelt* ; CV-42 was decommissioned after this deployment, which finished in April 1977, and VF-111 swapped its F-4Ns for more potent F-14As *(Michael Grove)*

Right Having completed his deck-level pre-flight walkaround, a young lieutenant with VF-142 'Ghostriders' briefly poses for the camera before climbing aboard 'his' jet in May 1974. The wonderful bone dome decoration on the pilot's helmet is typical of the colourful designs worn by aircrew of the period. Although some squadrons (notably VF-111) continue this practice today, the majority of frontline fighter units tend not to elaborately adorn their 'brain buckets' *(Angelo Romano)*

All three photographs featuring VF-143's colourful F-4Js were taken by the author during the squadron's one and only Med cruise with the Phantom II, which took place between January and August 1974. Unlike VF-142, the squadron chose not to alter their traditional blue and black scheme for this deployment. Wearing a CNO Safety 'S' on its splitter plate, this gleaming 'dog' comes back aboard ship following the successful completion of an ACM sortie over Sardinia. The overall appearance of VF-143's F-4Js during this cruise contrasts markedly with the squadron jet featured in the last chapter (*Angelo Romano*)

Many Navy squadrons flew the Phantom II during its lengthy period in frontline service, but few can boast having flown the original McDonnell Phantom as well. One of the select band of units to achieve the double is VF-154 'Black Knights', the squadron receiving the rather basic FH-1 Phantom whilst designated as reserve unit VF-837. Prior to receiving the McDonnell jet fighter, the unit had flown F6F-5 Hellcats and F4U-4/FG-1D Corsairs from its home at Floyd Bennett Field, NAS New York. These troublesome jets only featured on the squadron roster in 1950, a call up to active service following the outbreak of the Korean War resulting in the Phantoms making way for the far superior F9F-2 Panther. The Phantom II, however, wore VF-154's colours from November 1965 to November 1983. Seven years prior to their retirement date, these Phantom IIs were photographed at Miramar just two weeks before the squadron embarked aboard the

Ranger for a seven-month long WestPac cruise on 17 January 1976. The lead F-4J in this line-up wears the distinctive rainbow colours and 'Commander Attack Carrier Air Wing Two' titling which denotes that it is the squadron 'CAG Bird'. A close inspection of the canopy rail reveals that CVW-2's CAG on this cruise was none other than Cdr Sam Flynn Jnr, a legendary figure at NAS Oceana. Flynn had led VF-31 'Tomcatters' during their only WestPac in 1972/73, the squadron spending 173 days on the line. This cruise was a highly successful one for the unit as not a single F-4J was lost either in action or during routine flights. The highlight during the deployment was the MiG-21 kill scored by Flynn, and his RIO Lt William H John, on 21 June 1972; the fighter was claimed with an AIM-9 during a MiGCAP sortie *(Michael Grove)*

Five years later, VF-154's CAG aircraft wore no special markings to denote that it was the 'boss bird' other than the traditional 'double nuts (00) modex on the nose and fin tip. Photographed in May 1981 (just days away from a brief 'Pineapple Cruise' to Hawaii with CVW-14 aboard the Coral Sea), this jet had flown up to NAS Fallon with the rest of the air wing for the final pre-cruise work-ups over the Nevada ranges. This brief Pacific sailing enabled the squadron to familiarize itself with carrier ops once again following a 20-month hiatus in 'blue water' flying which had seen the unit transition to the F-4S from the F-4J, and then back to the F-4N following over the ramp speed problems with the Sierra model. Two WestPacs were completed by VF-154 aboard the venerable *Coral Sea* (1981/82 and 1983) before the 'Black Knights' finally retired their F-4Ns to Davis-Monthan AFB in October 1983, receiving factory-fresh F-14As in their place *(Michael Grove)*

VF-154's Phantom IIs wore the whole spectrum of colour schemes associated with the F-4 during the squadron's 18-year association with the jet. From fully blown glossy grey and white, detailed with gaudy black and red stripes, to lustreless two-tone grey, the 'Black Knights' experienced it all. This low-viz F-4N was photographed by the author at NAS Fallon trailing its drogue chute during a CVW-14 det in October 1982. For some unexplained reason the crew have taxied in with the jet's refuelling probe extended. Besides the near mandatory centreline tank, the only other ordnance carried by this F-4N is an AIM-9L dummy round, fitted with a fully operable infrared acquisition head which emits the familiar 'winder growl in the crew's headsets when it achieves a firing solution lock-on against its foe (*Michael Grove*)

Although VF-161 were responsible for the destruction of no less than six MiGs during the war in Vietnam, this particular jet was not involved in any of the sorties in question. Therefore, the small Vietnamese flag on its splitter plate must denote that the F-4N's pilot is the MiG killer, not the jet itself. Photographed on approach to the squadron's then new homebase at NAF Atsugi, this F-4N was one of 12 Phantom IIs assigned to the 'Chargers'. VF-161, and sister-squadron VF-151 'Vigilantes', were the last frontline US Navy units to retire the F-4, the squadrons flying their S-model jets directly from Japan to Davis-Monthan in 1986. During their 23-year association with the Phantom II, VF-161 operated all four major versions of

the F-4 at one time or another, flying from the decks of *Constellation*, *Coral Sea* and finally *Midway*. Transferred from the fighter to the light strike community upon their return to the USA in 1986, the 'Chargers' transitioned to the F/A-18A Hornet at NAS Lemoore, California, and eventually joined the newly established CVW-10. Redesignated VFA-161, the unit carrier qualified with the Hornet aboard the *Enterprise* during an at-sea period in July/August 1987, and was gearing itself up for an eventual WestPac aboard the newly refurbished USS *Independence* (CV-62) when budget cuts hit the Navy and both CVW-10 and VFA-161were disbanded *(Masumi Wada via Angelo Romano)*

Another squadron affected by CVW-10's disbandment was VF-194 'Red Lightnings', who, along with VF-191 'Satan's Kittens', were charged with providing fighter cover for the air wing in their F-14s. The squadron's brief life of 18 months mirrors its previous two-year association with the F-4J between April 1976 and March 1978. Then part of CVW-15, VF-194 and sister-squadron VF-191 had been the last frontline fighter squadrons to retire the F-8 Crusader from service, the units having flown the Vought fighter from 1959. Only one WestPac was completed by VF-194 following its re-equipment with the F-4J, the squadron taking its 'new' fighters aboard the *Coral Sea* on 15 February 1977. Prior to the deployment, four squadron jets were resprayed in the distinctive Keith Ferris camouflage scheme, which consisted of three shades of

grey (plus a false canopy on the aircraft's undersides); Federal Standards (FS) 36321 (dark grey), 36440 (gull grey) and 36622 (light grey). The overall results of the trial were; '1. the scheme increased the initial detection range of the aircraft because of high visual reflectance contrast of the colours; 2. the false canopy was effective in causing deception of the observer; 3. the pattern did not cause deception; 4. upon continual exposure to the scheme the false canopy was less effective in causing deception'. So wrote Lt Mark Morgan in his excellent article entitled 'Where has all the colour gone?', published in *Tail Hook* magazine in the Fall 1987 edition. Although the shades were toned down in mid-1977, the scheme was not chosen *(Peter Marcus via Angelo Romano)*

Most frontline Navy types eventually end their days with the reserve, refurbished and issued to one of the many part-time units scattered across the USA. All four fighter squadrons assigned to the reserve received F-4Bs and Ns in the mid-1970s as replacements for their clapped out F-8J Crusaders. Wearing some of the most colourful schemes ever seen on the Phantom II, these veteran jets fulfilled the fighter duties for the Atlantic Fleet's Reserve Carrier Air Wing 20 (CVWR-20) and the Pacific Fleet's Reserve Carrier Air Wing 30 (CVWR-30) for over ten years, before finally being replaced by the Tomcat. Basking in the sun at its NAS Dallas, Texas, homebase, this typically pristine F-4N was photographed between sorties in May 1978 wearing the distinctive markings of VF-201 'Hunters'. Prior to the advent of low-viz markings, the 'Hunters' derived their squadron colours from those worn on the state flag *(Michael Grove)*

Right By 1980, the colours of the flag had been replaced by a map of the 'Lone Star' state itself, VF-201 still defying the CNO directive by flanking 'Texas' with a pair of blood red fin flashes. The overall grey shade worn on this F-4N is FS 16440, a colour chosen by the CNO in February 1977 as an interim shade for use whilst the definitive Tactical Paint Scheme (TPS) for naval aircraft was developed. This shade was rapidly applied to fighter aircraft in order to eradicate the visual cues given to an adversary by the old gull grey on insignia white scheme (*Michael Grove*)

Above Four years later, and now equipped with the F-4S, VF-201 had totally succumbed to the TPS scheme, although this jet was still carrying a glossy grey centreline tank when photographed at Fallon in August 1984. Along with the matt greys came the luminescent formation lighting strips affixed to the aircraft's nose, fuselage and tail. Wearing both a Battle 'E' and a Safety 'S' on its splitter plate, this F-4S sits quietly on the ramp awaiting its crew, having already been bombed up by the squadron's armourers prior to the morning's Alpha strike on the Bravo 17 range. The three 'cookies' on the port triple ejector rack are Mk 82 500 lb General Purpose (GP) bombs, primed with standard fuzes (*Michael Grove*)

VF-201's sister-squadron within CVWR-20 is VF-202 'Superheats', and like the 'Rangers', they have progressed from the Crusader, through several models of the Phantom II to the Tomcat. The reserve crews of both units contributed the closing 'blue water' chapter to the Phantom II story when they completed the final carqual period for the venerable fighter in October 1986 aboard the *America* as the carrier sailed off the coast of Virginia. During May of 1985, VF-201 and -202 flew cross-country to NAS Fallon and joined up with elements of both reserve wings for two-weeks of solid strike warfare training over the vast instrumented weapons ranges that form three-quarters of the base. Taxying out at the beginning of yet another ACM sortie, this drab F-4S carries a Cubic Corporation TACTS (Tactical Air Combat Training System) pod on its port TER, this device monitoring the aircraft's airspeed, altitude, angle of attack, attitude and simulated weapons status instantaneously, and transmitting the data in real time back to the Naval Strike Warfare Center HQ, via microwave telemetry. At the time of VF-202's visit, the TACTs was still being integrated into Naval Aviation's overall air wing training programme, the first SLATS (Strike Leader Attack Training Syllabus) course having only been completed eight months before *(Michael Grove via Angelo Romano)*

Above As mentioned earlier in this chapter, the reserve units at Miramar were the beneficiaries of the F-4S/*Coral Sea* problem that beset VF-21 and -154 just prior to their first WestPac with the ultimate Navy Phantom II. The first F-4Ss arrived at VF-302 in the early summer of 1981, their migration along the Miramar flightline to 'Reserve Country' being mirrored by a similar movement of F-4Ns in the opposite direction towards the hangar spaces of CVW-14's fighter squadrons. VF-302's first det with the F-4S saw them heading inland for Fallon, and two weeks of bombing and ACM work in the Sierra Nevadas. Configured in true 'Fallon ACM' guise (no centreline tank), this 'CAG bird' has two empty TERs affixed to its wing hardpoints, signalling the successful completion of a live bombing sortie over Bravo 17. Parked behind the F-4S is a veteran RF-8G of CVWR-30's VFP-306 'Peeping Toms', the Crusader being readied for a post-strike recce flight over the range *(Michael Grove)*

Left On the West Coast, the reserve fighter duties are performed by VF-301 'Devil's Disciples' and VF-302 'Stallions', these gaudily marked F-4Ss hailing from the latter unit. All three jets wear the reincarnated Ferris greys, although this time the angles and shades had been applied with the advice of experienced naval aviator Lt Cdr (now Cdr) C J 'Heater' Heatley, of *Cutting Edge* fame, firmly in mind. Only the reserve Phantom II units at Miramar wore this Heater-Ferris scheme, and after a thorough evaluation AirPac submitted an Operational Requirement to the CNO requesting approval for it to apply the four shades of grey to its aircraft. This request was denied in May 1984, the CNO stating that 'It does not appear that the proposed paint scheme would have significant benefits over the current tactical paint scheme when considering all environmental conditions and flight profiles.' These jets were photographed soon after they had been resprayed in the experimental scheme in October 1982 during CVWR-30's carqual period aboard the *Constellation* (McDonnell Douglas photo)

Enter the Tomcat

Unlike the Phantom II, which wore glossy markings for two-thirds of its operational career, Grumman's F-14 Tomcat has now been afflicted with TPS greys for well over half of its frontline service life. Some squadrons have managed to introduce a small amount of colour within their individual markings to brighten up the aircraft a little, but VF-11 'Red Rippers' are not amongst their number! This heavily mottled jet was photographed high over the Med as it tanked from a buddy refuelling pod slung under the wing of a VA-37 'Bulls' A-7E Corsair II; both aircraft were embarked aboard USS *Forrestal* (CV-59) as part of CVW-6 for the carrier's six-month Med cruise which lasted from November 1989 to April 1990. During the deployment, CVW-6 accumulated 16,000 flight hours, logged a total of 6752 traps and achieved a mission completion rate of 98.5 per cent. Following the completion of *Forrestal*'s final Med cruise in December 1991, CVW-6 was disestablished and its squadrons either stood down or transferred to the Pacific Fleet. One unit experiencing the latter was VF-11, who (along with sister-squadron VF-31 'Tomcatters') have moved to Miramar and are currently transitioning onto the ultimate Tomcat, the F-14D *(Lt(jg) Brian Herdlick via Angeo Romano)*

Sixteen years prior to *Forrestal*'s final Med cruise, sister Atlantic Fleet carrier USS *John F Kennedy* (CV-67) sailed east across the Atlantic with 20 brand new Tomcats on its flightdeck. Part of CVW-1, and marked up in either full VF-14 'Tophatters' or VF-32 'Swordsmen' squadron colours, the F-14As were making their debut with the 6th Fleet. Departing Norfolk on 28 June 1975 and remaining on station until the following January, VF-14 was participating in its first 'blue water' deployment since the squadron's final tour with the F-4B in 1973 (again aboard the 'JFK'). All of 1974 and the early months of 1975 were spent working up with the new Tomcats, initially with VF-124 at Miramar and then back at VF-14's home base at Oceana. To celebrate the Tomcat's introduction to the East Coast fighter community, both VF-14 and VF-32 chose schemes which reached new heights in gaudiness. The 'Tophatters' chose red (their traditional colour) as the backdrop for their famous 'High Hat' emblem, the squadron's F-14s being liberally covered with scarlet paint. The ultimate statement in VF-14 aircraft art was F-14A BuNo 159424, this Tomcat serving as the squadron's replacement 'CAG bird' following the loss of their original boss machine (BuNo 159007), which overran the flight deck due to an arrestor gear failure whilst landing aboard the 'JFK' on 5 August 1975 in the Med; VF-14 used miniature chevrons sprayed up in rainbow colours to mark its CAG aircraft (*Angelo Romano*)

Above The squadron's elaborate markings only lasted a single Med cruise however, VF-14's next 6th Fleet sailing aboard 'JFK' in 1977 seeing its Tomcats devoid of most colour, but still wearing the black 'High Hat' on its twin fins. Following two more deployments with CV-67 in the late 1970s, VF-14 was reassigned to CVW-6, and after a 14-month shorebased training cycle embarked aboard the *Independence* for the carrier's inaugural Tomcat cruise in late 1982. VF-14's partnership with CVW-6 and the 'Indy' lasted until 1 April 1985 when the squadron joined CVW-3 and reacquainted itself with 'JFK's' flightdeck once again; as this book went to press VF-14 was still assigned to CVW-3 and CV-67 (*US Navy photo*)

Left Unlike most other AirLant fighter units, VF-31 'Tomcatters' have somehow managed to bend the no colour CNO directive to allow its F-14s to wear solid red fins and virtually gloss black radomes! Photographed just seconds before trucking down *Forrestal'* s bow cat two during a NATO exercise in the eastern Mediterranean in September 1986, this Tomcat carries a mixture of external stores. Mounted to its port shoulder missile rail is an AIM-9M Sidewinder and an AIM-7M Sparrow, whilst nestled between the two 267-gal external tanks beneath the fuselage is a Tactical Air Reconnaissance Pod System (TARPS) (*Angelo Romano*)

Above 'Showboating, VF-31 style!'. When photographed during the *Ocean Safari* exercise in September 1983, these two 'Tomcatters' were assigned to CVW-3 aboard the 'JFK'. The squadron received its first F-14As at Oceana in August 1980, and following a strenuous period of training and work-ups with VF-101 deployed with CVW-3 to the Med in January 1982 aboard the *Kennedy*. During this inaugural 6th Fleet cruise, the squadron supported Navy operations off the coast of Lebanon, flying many successful TARPS missions over the beleaguered nation. Although transferred to CVW-6 and *Forrestal* in 1985, VF-31 held onto its colourful markings through to the early 1990s. Like former sister-squadron VF-11, the 'Tomcatters' have recently moved to Miramar and are currently working up on the F-14D
(*US Navy photo*)

Right The catapult crew signal to the 'shooter' that both jetpipes have dilated fully and that the twin Pratt & Whitney TF30-P414A turbofans have kicked into afterburner. By this stage in the prelaunch sequence the pilot will have already checked his flying surfaces by vigorously deploying the wing spoilers and cycling the all-moving tailplanes up and down, before depressing them slightly below the horizontal for launch. Like most other VF-31 jets on this 1986 Med cruise, 'Tomcatter 207' wears full squadron colours, which have been applied onto an overall glossy gull grey (FS 16440) shade
(*Angelo Romano*)

Right As mentioned earlier in this chapter, VF-14's partners during the Tomcat's first 6th Fleet cruise were VF-32 'Swordsmen' who, in keeping with CVW-I's colourful tradition, sprayed their F-14s up in the most shocking shade of gold that could be found in the Oceana paint store. With the sun low in the west, the Tomcat tails dominate the deck of 'JFK' as the carrier prepares to launch its next cycle of jets in November 1975. Although the CO's jet in the foreground is fully manned, the gear leg chains and the wheel chocks are still firmly in place. Ranged up alongside the factory fresh Tomcat is an equally new Grumman EA-6B Prowler of VAQ-133 'Wizards'; following almost two decades of electronic warfare operations, VAQ-133 was disestablished in 1992 after completing its final Med cruise with CVW-6 aboard the *Forrestal (Angelo Romano)*

Above Looking good for an 'OK-3 underlined grade' trap back aboard CV-67, the XO's Tomcat glides past a pair of S-3A Vikings of VS-21 'Fighting Redtails' and a single VF-32 F-14A, before snagging a wire and rapidly decelerating on the greasy deck. Both F-14s wear a distinctive gold number one beneath the RIO's 'office' which denotes that VF-32 were the Admiral Joseph Clifton Award winners for 1974/75. This highly sought after trophy is bestowed upon the fighter squadron which maintains both the highest level of battle efficiency and the best safety record over a 12-month period. The competition is open to squadrons from both coasts. The Tomcat spotted in the background (BuNo 159022) was lost on 5 December 1979 (whilst assigned to VF-14) when it collided with another squadron jet (BuNo 160902) near Roosevelt Roads, Puerto Rico, and crashed into the Caribbean; the latter jet managed to land safely *(Angelo Romano)*

During its early years in fleet
service, the Tomcat rarely flew with
external stores, bar the occasional
dummy AIM-9 Sidewinder round
on a shoulder pylon; this VF-32 jet
carries only the streamlined AIM-54
Phoenix missile pallets beneath its
fuselage. The rigours of five months
at sea are beginning to show on this
once pristine Tomcat, its fuselage
avionics equipment bay panels
exhibiting blotches of rust inhibitor
on many of the airframe fasteners.
Further patches of primer appear on
the wing leading-edges and on the
lower fuselage intakes
(*Angelo Romano*)

Left Ten years later, all the glorious colour of the mid-1970s had been totally replaced by the TPS greys. Although still aboard the 'JFK', VF-32 now wore CVW-3's 'AC' tailcodes in places of CVW-l's 'AB'; the 'Swordsmen' had also spent three years wearing CVW-6's 'AE' codes aboard the *Independence* between 1982 and 1985. This veteran Tomcat still has the old wide-fairing 'beaver tail' unit between the jet nozzles. Virtually all F-14s in service today have the cut-down fairing, which has no fillets on either side of the ECM antenna or the fuel dump valve. The squadron was enjoying a brief portcall in Naples in January 1987 (at the end of strenuous Med cruise) when this photograph was taken. During the deployment VF-32 (as part of CVW-3) had exercised with NATO forces during *Display Determination 86*, the Egyptians in *Seawind*, the Spanish in *Poopdeck* and with the Navy and Air Force of Morocco during exercise *African Eagle (Angelo Romano)*

Above On 4 January 1989 two F-14s from VF-32 splashed a pair of Libyan MiG-23MS *Flogger E*s that were approaching 'JFK's' battlegroup as it sailed through the Med in international waters. These kills were the first MiGs claimed by American aircraft since the final days of the Vietnam war, and up to the end of 1992 were still the only Mikoyan Gurevich fighters destroyed by the US Navy since 1973. Eighteen months and two Med cruises later, this colourful Tomcat was spotted on the ramp at Oceana wearing full unit colours and two MiG silhouettes beneath the cockpit. BuNo 162694 was not involved in the action however, (BuNos 159437 and 159610 were credited with the kills), and neither was its allocated pilot, squadron boss Cdr George 'Chip' Slaven. VF-32 is currently still assigned to CVW-3 and the Kennedy (*via Angelo Romano*).

Above With the cat shot over, the pilot regains control of his 'Starfighter' and pulls the nose of the jet up as the F-14A climbs away from *America*'s deck. The Alpha model's twin TF30s produce 20,900 lbs of thrust each when in full afterburner, which on paper appears to be a very impressive figure. However, a fuelled up Tomcat with a mix of missiles or a TARPS pod, can leave the deck with a total weight of up to 74,349 lbs, thus giving the F-14A a thrust-to-weight ratio that is well below the much coveted pound per pound figure that most designers strive to achieve (*US Navy photo*)

Left Having climbed above the thick cloud, which appears to stretch out in all directions, a lone VF-33 'Starfighters' F-14A hooks up with a VA-34 "Blue Blasters' KA-6D mid way through a CAP in support of *America*'s battlegroup. Once its tanks have been topped off the Tomcat will return to its patrol line 100 miles ahead of the carrier. This routine JP4 transaction was photographed by Lt Cdr Dave 'Hey Joe' Parsons, who was serving as RIO in a second F-14, during VF-33's first full 6th Fleet deployment. Originally known as the 'Tarsiers' (named after a small, ferocious fox-like mammal from Africa), VF-33 was initially established as a Hellcat unit in the Solomon Islands in 1943. Disbanded following the cessation of hostilities, the squadron was re-established with the Bearcat at Quonset Point, Rhode Island, on 12 October 1948. However, by the time it went into action over Korea in August 1950, VF-33 had exchanged its F8Fs for F4U-4 Corsairs. Following several war cruises, the unit converted to the F9F-6 Cougar in 1959. The decade ended with two Med cruises aboard *Intrepid* equipped with the F11F-1 Tiger, this less than successful Grumman fighter being replaced by the F8U-lE Crusader in 1961. VF-33's seemingly endless re-equipment with a succession of new types finally ended in November 1964 when the squadron began converting onto the F-4B at Key West; the 'Starfighters' flew B-models until 1968, and S-models up to 1981. VF-33 are currently still equipped with the F-14A and maintain their place within CVW-1 aboard the *America* – in fact VF-33 have never operated the Tomcat from any other carrier, or with any other air wing! (*Lt Cdr Dave 'Hey Joe' Parsons via Angelo Romano*)

Above Along with VF-31 'Tomcatters', the 'Black Aces' of VF-41 were the only other squadron in the Navy to carry over their traditional black radomes from the Phantom II to the Tomcat, although unlike the former unit, VF-41's jets only wore this scheme for a single Med cruise. Associated with the F-4 from 1962 through to 1976, the 'Black Aces' first deployed with their new Tomcats to the Med aboard the equally new USS *Nimitz* (CVN-68) in December 1977. Photographed over the Italian Alps five months into the inaugural cruise, this early production F-14A wears full squadron markings, including the distinctive rank tab flashes on the cockpit coaming. Like other F-14s of the period, the aircraft is devoid of missiles or external fuel tanks. At this stage in the Tomcat's service life the aircraft carried only an AN/ALQ-126 deception jamming transmitter and a collision beacon beneath its radome *(via Angelo Romano)*

Left When the squadron next headed out to sea in September 1979, VF-41's black noses and red and white tails had gone, only the traditional insignia white undersides and full colour roundels hinting at past glory days. By the early 1980s even they had been replaced, although the squadron still managed to add a small red stripe on their twin fins in an act of open defiance to CNO directives! During VF-41's third 6th Fleet deployment a pair of squadron jets (including one flown by head 'Black Ace' Cdr Henry 'Hank' Kleeman) engaged two Libyan Sukhoi Su-22 *Fitter Js* over the Gulf of Sidra following an aggressive missile shoot at the Tomcats. Both *Fitter Js* were splashed in under a minute by a pair of AIM-9Ls after a brief textbook engagement. Photographed soon after this rather one-sided tussle, these heavily armed F-14As are seen patrolling at height over the Med late in the 1981/82 cruise. Following this remarkable tour of duty, VF-41 was awarded the Clifton Trophy, plus the CNO Safety 'S' and the ComNavAirLant Battle Efficiency 'E' in early 1982 *(US Navy photo)*

Left By the late 1980s most Tomcat operators had taken full advantage of the CNO's new ruling which allowed both the CAG aircraft and the CO's mount to be adorned in full unit markings if the squadron boss so wished. VF-41 didn't have to be told twice! The sole gloss grey aircraft on the squadron books was quickly resprayed with an attractive card motif on its twin fins, and a long anti-glare strip was applied to the top of the radome and back past the canopy onto the rear fuselage. The squadron has maintained its allegiance to CVW-8 for over 16 years, and transferred with the wing to the then new USS *Theodore Roosevelt* (CVN-71) in 1987 following the relocation of the *Nimitz* to the West Coast *(Angelo Romano)*

Above Framed by thunderous clouds, a pristine VF-51 'Screaming Eagles' Tomcat rolls down the long Fallon parallel taxyway prior to commencing a brief ACM sortie out over the ranges. Wearing horizontal rainbow CAG stripes on its tail in place of the traditional red ones, this pristine jet is painted up in period early 1980s squadron markings – only the small grey star and bar hints at the drabness that was to follow for VF-51 as the decade progressed *(Michael Grove)*

Above To break up the monotony of TPS greys, several squadrons have experimented with Tactical Watercolour Camouflage (TWC) throughout the 1980s, these one-off schemes appearing in response to specific threat requirements experienced during *Red Flag* and Fallon deployments. Some squadrons like VF-1 'Wolfpack' liberally daubed their aircraft in bright blue paint, while some attack units opted for several shades of tan and brown in order to allow their jets to blend in with desert backdrops during low-level strike missions. These schemes have usually appeared immediately prior to a training evolution or exercise det, and are normally removed during routine corrosion prevention cleaning back at the squadron's home station. Wearing unit markings that are barely discernible, this blotchy VF-51 Tomcat was photographed at Fallon in 1987 camouflaged in a curious mix of colours. Bolted onto the hardpoint is a TACTS pod and a finless Sidewinder acquisition round, the latter device giving the crew the 'bark' of the AIM-9, but not the 'bite *(Michael Grove)*

Right Since the advent of the TPS, squadrons have not had to try too hard to make their aircraft look old and shabby. These VF-74 Tomcats, stacked side by side aboard *Saratoga* in May 1984, were virtually new when this photograph was taken during the squadron's first Mediterranean cruise with the F-14, yet they look as if they could be ready for a one-way flight to Davis-Monthan. The stained and patchy appearance of the paint reveals just how porous the TPS is, its rough texture absorbing dirt and grease from both the maintenance crews and the flightdeck. The actual scheme itself should consist of three shades of grey, although touch up painting, incorrect shades and variable weathering all soon collaborate to destroy any tactical benefit originally offered by the TPS. The squadrons themselves are restricted by CNO regulations concerning aircraft respraying. These directives firmly state that no overall repainting of airframes can be attempted at anything less than depot level, and that the 'TPS will not be changed without official approval'. The squadrons can touch up the scheme in the following areas: the BuNo; safety, egress, warning and access markings; squadron identification; type aircraft; national insignia; unit identification (vertical fin); branch of service; side numbers; and squadron insignia in a single TPS grey shade, which is not to exceed an area of 1000 square inches *(Angelo Romano)*

Above 'Super Sara' plows gently through the eastern Mediterranean during its first 6th Fleet deployment since the completion of its SLEP (Service Life Extension Program) in early 1984. The carrier had been laid up in Philadelphia Navy Yard for two and a half years whilst its internal compartments were modernized and its catapult equipment reworked to allow the vessel to operate Tomcats from its flightdeck. The second of four *Forrestal* class carriers built for the Navy, *Saratoga* was commissioned on 14 April 1956, and has served exclusively during its 36 years of 'blue water' ops with the Atlantic Fleet. *Saratoga* was the first carrier to undergo the SLEP modernization, which is aimed at keeping the older vessels in service past the turn of the century *(US Navy photo)*

Left Twelve months later, VF-74 was once again at sea operating in warm Mediterranean waters. The markings worn during this cruise were identical to those carried on the first trip, the squadron's only splash of colour consisting of a scarlet lightning bolt which pierced the devil motif on the twin fins. During this deployment VF-74, along with other squadrons under the control of CVW-17, made international headlines when four Tomcats intercepted an Egyptian Boeing 737 heading for Libya that was carrying four terrorists involved in the hijacking of the Italian cruise liner *Achille Lauro*. The fighters guided the 737 to the US Navy base at Sigonella, on the island of Sicily, where the terrorists were arrested by Italian authorities. Today, VF-74 are still with CVW-17 and the *Saratoga*, although now the squadron flies the re-engined F-14B Tomcat *(Angelo Romano)*

Of all the schemes worn by the first units to transition onto the Tomcat in the mid-1970s, VF-84's combination of black, gold and a grisly skull to top it all off, is perhaps the best remembered. After all, who could forget the legendary dogfight scene between a pair of 'Jolly Rogers'' F-14s (dangerously close to stalling speed) and a dastardly brace of A6M 'Texan' Zeroes out over the Pacific during that immortal Hollywood epic of 1980, *The Final Countdown*. Five years prior to their celluloid heroics in July 1975, the 'Jolly Rogers' had just returned to Oceana after completing their final 6th Fleet cruise with the weary F-4N aboard the *Roosevelt*. Three months later the squadron prepared for re-equipment, although the

last Phantom II didn't leave the unit until March 1976 and formal crew training with VF-101 on the Tomcat only commenced the following June. By mid-April 1977 the squadron was ready for action, and was duly reassigned to CVW-8; this wing still controls VF-84 today. One of the first duties performed by the 'Jolly Rogers' was to respray their brand new Tomcats in traditional squadron colours, the scheme eventually adopted by VF-84 being almost identical to that worn on their recently retired F-4Ns. BuNo 160397 was photographed by the author in February 1978 as the squadron sailed aboard the *Nimitz* in the Med during VF-84's first 6th Fleet cruise (*Angelo Romano*)

Left By February 1982 the only insignia white remaining on VF-84's Tomcats picked out the full-size skull and crossbones on the twin fins and the miniature star and bar within the national insignia. Photographed high above the clouds during one of the last dusk patrols of the cruise whilst on-station with the 6th Fleet, this jet is armed up with a live AIM-7M Sparrow missile on the port rail. Although sister-squadron VF-41 gained notoriety during this deployment for splashing two Libyan Su-22s, VF-84 made history in its own right by becoming the first fleet unit to utilize the TARPS equipment on an operational cruise. The squadron first received training on the new recce system with VF-124 'Gunfighters' at Miramar, three pods then arriving at VF-84 just prior to the cruise in July 1981. The system worked beautifully and the pods were duly cleared for fleet use *(via Angelo Romano)*

Above VF-84 managed to stave off the TPS longer than most other Tomcat squadrons, although the unit eventually succumbed to the inevitable in early 1986. The end result was a squadron of distinctively marked F-14s, VF-84 retaining their former insignia, although this time sprayed on in varying shades of grey. Photographed during the squadron's first Med cruise aboard the new *Theodore Roosevelt* in February 1989, this low-viz 'Jolly Roger' wears a distinctive mid-fuselage demarcation line between the two TPS shades; this peculiar marking has been a feature of VF-84's Tomcats of late. Heavily involved in a variety of support missions protecting CVW-8's strike assets during *Operation Desert Storm*, VF-84 also performed a series of TARPS missions during *Operation Provide Comfort*, the squadron overseeing the relief operations carried out in northern Iraq for the Kurdish refugees
(via Angelo Romano)

Prominently displaying their training modexs (and a variety of TPS colours), these weary Tomcats all belong to VF-101 Det Key West. Along with their replacement air group counterparts, VF-124 'Gunfighters' at Miramar, VF-101 operate the largest fleet of Tomcats in the Navy. Up to 20 aircraft are permanently on the squadron books, the fighters accruing more flying hours in a shorter period of time than any frontline fleet airframes. Operating the venerable A-model, the halfway house Bravo and the ultimate Tomcat, the F-14D, VF-101 split their assets between their permanent home at Oceana and the fine-weather det at Key West. Originally activated at Cecil Field, Florida, on 1 May 1952 as part of CVG-10, the 'Grim Reapers' flew Banshees, Skyrays, Demons and Skyknights before commencing the replacement carrier air group role with the F4H-1 Phantom II in June 1960. Based at Key West from 1958 until 1971, the squadron eventually moved back up to Oceana, although an F-4 det was maintained in Florida (designated VF-171 Detachment Key West in August 1977). This move better reflected the split that had taken place at Oceana with the arrival of the F-14, the main body of VF-101 being responsible for the training of Tomcat pilots and RIOs after August 1977. All F-4 training was then taken over by VF-171 'Aces' at Oceana. After VF-171 was deactivated in June 1984, the 'Grim Reapers' only used Key West for short detachments. However, on 27 June 1989 the 'Reapers' returned to Florida in force, activating a permanent VF-101 Det Key West with 10 Tomcats, 16 officers and 195 enlisted personnel (*Angelo Romano*)

Above Brute force gets the job done! A groundcrew team from VF-101 uplift a dummy Sidewinder round into place on the port shoulder pylon of a 'Grim Reapers' F-14A spotted out on the Key West ramp. The 'missile' is fitted with a live acquisition head, which will be uncaged and aligned prior to the sortie being flown. Inboard of the Sidewinder is a cubic Corporation Air Combat Manoeuvring Instrumentation (ACMI) pod; both devices combine out over the instrumented Dry Tortugas ACM range off Florida's coast to provide the ultimate in training scenarios for budding fighter crews transitioning onto the Tomcat with VF-101 *(Angelo Romano)*

Right Chasing the rapidly setting sun as it descends over the Sierra Nevada Mountains, a colourful pair of Tomcats from VF-102 'Diamondbacks' pose in tight echelon right formation for 'Hey Joe' Parsons' camera during a squadron det to Fallon in December 1983. A close inspection of the BuNos reveals that these aircraft were built side by side on the Bethpage production line several years before, and that both F-14s have been wired up for TARPS compatibility; VF-102 were actually the Oceana 'TARPS TOPGUNS' at the time this photograph was taken, which was no mean feat when you consider that the unit had only been equipped with the Tomcat since May 1982. Since the establishment of the 'Strike U' at Fallon in late 1984, a comprehensive TARPS training course has been available for visiting air wings, the two-phase curriculum seeing the designated recce unit flying 12 day and 12 night sorties at low-level over a variety of routes and targets in various scenarios. All flights are fully co-ordinated through the NSWC, and the TARPS course is usually conducted very early on in the wing's 18-day schedule *(Lt Cdr Dave 'Hey Joe' Parsons via Angelo Romano)*

Above The Tomcat's 24-hour capability has been thoroughly used by the Navy over the years, squadrons performing around-the-clock BarCAP patrols in defence of the carrier, and its battlegroup, in virtually any weather (*Lt Cdr Dave 'Hey Joe' Parsons via Angelo Romano*)

Above right Producing photography as sharp as this it is not surprising that VF-102 'Diamondbacks' won the Atlantic Fleet TARPS prize in 1983/84. Using the pod's KA-93 panoramic camera (fitted amidships), the crew of a suitably modified F-14 snapped this highly detailed image of their 'home' (*America*) as it sailed through the Med during the carrier's 6th Fleet deployment in 1984. The KA-93 system has since been replaced by the more advanced Fairchild KA-99 panoramic camera, which allows the crew to cover an even wider area. In the nose of the pod is a CAI KS-87B single-frame camera which operates obliquely through a slanted flat-pane window. Finally, to allow the crew to complete sorties 24 hours a day in the worst weather, a Honeywell AN/AAD-5 infrared linescan system has also been housed within the TARPS (*US Navy Photo*)

Right Slimming down to a safe landing weight, a VF-102 Tomcat vents JP4 out of its large fuel dump pipe prior to making a hook down, low-level pass over the *America* in October 1984. Once the fighter has buzzed the carrier, its pilot will perform a hard 'bad to the bone' five-G break to port and enter the recovery pattern, cycling the landing gear out and selecting forward sweep for the wings. The 'Diamondbacks' were one of the last Oceana-based fighter squadrons to retire the Phantom II, the unit having since made up for its late transition with an unbroken series of 6th Fleet cruises with CVW-1 and the *America* (*Lt Cdr Dave 'Hey Joe' Parsons via Angelo Romano*)

Squadrons and carriers often maintain close links over many years of service, the vessel's flightdeck charting the development of a unit as it periodically transitions to more advanced equipment. One such association that is now entering its third decade is the VF-103 'Sluggers' / USS *Saratoga* (CV-60) partnership, the Oceana-based fighter squadron having first embarked on the 'Super Sara' with F-4Bs as part of CVW-3 in March 1966. Over the next 14 years the 'Sluggers' successfully completed ten 6th Fleet cruises and a single WestPac deployment aboard the carrier, the squadron transitioning onto the F-4J in 1968 during a break between cruises. The links between the squadron and CV-60 were temporarily severed at the end of 1980 as the carrier headed for Philadelphia Navy Yard for its extensive SLEP. VF-103, meanwhile, transitioned to the F-4S and was reassigned to CVW-17, which embarked aboard the *Forrestal* for a routine Med cruise in May 1982. Back at Oceana in November, VF-103 finally discarded the Phantom II for the Tomcat, the squadron successfully completing its work-ups just in time to rejoin the *Saratoga* following its overhaul. Photographed at rest during the carrier's very first post-refit cruise in August 1984, this glossy Tomcat was one of only a handful of 'Sluggers'' jets on deployment not wearing full TPS colours
(Carlo Tripodi via Angelo Romano)

The RIO watches the catapult crew hiding in the trough that surrounds the flightdeck as the pilot prepares to cycle the nozzles outwards and select afterburner for launch. The huge slab of deck known as the jet blast deflector (JBD) is firmly locked in place behind the Tomcat; this device will direct the scorching nozzle gases up and over the parked jets lined up behind the catapult awaiting their turn to launch. VF-103 was one of the first fleet units to transition onto the re-engined F-14B in mid-1989, the 'Sluggers' taking their 'new' jets to war in the Gulf aboard the *Saratoga* during Desert Storm. Flying hundreds of CAP and TARPS sorties in support of CVW-17, VF-103 was the only Tomcat squadron involved in the conflict to lose an aircraft to enemy fire; BuNo 161430, crewed by Lt Devon Jones (pilot) and Lt Larry Slade (RIO), was hit by an SA-2 missile at 26,000 feet while escorting a single EA-6B of VAQ-132, which was performing a HARM mission near the Iraqi airfield at Al Asad on 21 January 1991. Both crewmen ejected safely, Jones being rescued some hours later by a USAF special forces MH-53J, whilst Slade was captured and interned until the Iraqi ceasefire in March (*Angelo Romano*)

The lengthy relationships enjoyed by many East Coast fighter squadrons with Atlantic Fleet carriers are rarely encountered on the West Coast, units tending to swap carriers on a regular basis as the CVs and CVNs are periodically sent 'back east' for SLEPs. Occasionally a squadron will encounter a familiar flightdeck that was its home a decade or two before. For example, VF-111 'Sundowners' and USS *Kitty Hawk* (CV-63) have shared experiences over four decades now, the squadron first embarking on the carrier in the autumn of 1962, soon after receiving F8U-2N Crusaders. Following another 7th Fleet cruise in 1963/64, the unit moved to CVW-2 and the *Midway*. Fifteen years were to pass before the squadron reacquainted itself with the *Kitty Hawk* once again, VF-111 embarking with CVW-15 for its first WestPac with the F-14 in May 1979. Only one other deployment was made with CV-63, VF-111 then transferring to the then brand new nuclear carrier USS *Carl Vinson* (CVN-70) in March 1983. Photographed at Fallon in October 1982, this immaculate Tomcat (BuNo 160660) wears full 'Sundowners' colours and CVW-15's 'NL' tailcode, but is devoid of any carrier titling *(Michael Grove)*

Above Illustrating the variety of schemes worn by the squadron at the time, 'Sundowner 207' was one of the first VF-111 jets to wear full TPS greys, its sinister appearance at Fallon in October 1982 being a sign of the bleak, colourless future that was soon to embrace the unit. The relative newness of the scheme is illustrated by the glossy Phoenix missile pallets fitted to the jet's centreline, and the simil.arly marked external rails bolted inboard of the engine intakes *(Michael Grove)*

Right Photographed at Fallon during tne same weapons det was BuNo 160666, alias VF-111's highly colourful 'CAG bird'. This aircraft served as the squadron's 'senior' airframe from VF-111's first days with the Tomcat through to December 1982, when it was sent to the NARF at North Island for a major overhaul. Initially, the aircraft wore the sunburst in miniature on its ventral fins, and only carried the 'NL' codes on its twin tails. At that time, the CAG markings consisted of nine small stars on the starboard rudder and ten aircraft silhouettes on the port moving surface. The sunburst eventually made an appearance in 1981, the squadron's initial design seeing the 'meatball' positioned at the base of the fins' leading edges. This motif was soon modified however, the sun being moved aft to the centre of the fins . The traditional CAG colours were then applied in thin lines to the edges of the red rays *(Michael Grove)*

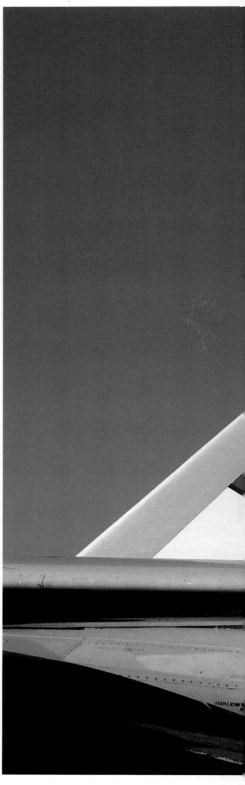

Left By 1986, VF-111's tail markings had been modified yet again and the squadron 'CAG bird' was none other than BuNo 160660, a veteran Tomcat that had heen with the 'Sundowners' since the unit transitioned onto the F-14A back in 1978. Photographed here escorting a Soviet Tupolev Tu-95 *Bear* high over the South China Sea, this jet wears the distinctive Superman motif below the 'front office',denoting that its pilot is none other than the original 'Super CAG' himself, Capt (now Rear Admiral) Ron 'Zap' Zlatoper. VF-111 and the *Kitty Hawk* were united once again in October 1991 as CVW-15 embarked aboard the recently refurbished CV-63 for the carriers two-month long positioning cruise around Cape Horn to San Diego. Although the squadron was due to transition onto the F-14D in 1991, these plans have been postponed indefinitely due to air wing reshuffling and severe budget restrictions *(US Navy photo)*

Above Another squadron with ties to the *Kitty Hawk* is VF-114 'Aardvarks', the squadron making no less than ten WestPac deployments both in war and peace between 1964 and 1975 aboard CV-63 whilst equipped with the F-4 Phantom II. Like VF-111, the 'Aardvarks'' first cruise with the Tomcat was performed aboard the *Kitty Hawk*, the squadron deploying with its traditional controlling body, CVW-11, to the Pacific in October 1977. After this solitary WestPac, the air wing moved to the *America* and performed two Med cruises in an effort to rectify the imbalance in the number of large-deck carrier wings assigned to the Atlantic Fleet. Four years after its last WestPac, VF-114 finally returned to the Pacific Fleet when CVW-11 was reassigned to the recently refurbished *Enterprise*; the unit embarked for its first cruise in September 1982. Looking resplendent in full squadron colours, and armed up with live short and medium range missiles, this 'Aardvark' was photographed by roving RIO Lt Cdr Dave 'Hey Joe' Parsons during a BarCAP over thick cloud whilst the *Enterprise* was on 'Gonzo Station' at the mouth of the Persian Gulf in November 1982 *(Lt Cdr Dave 'Hey Joe' Parsons via Angelo Romano)*

Above Having completed its first post-refit WestPac with flying colours in April 1983, the *Enterprise* then spent 12 months sailing in local waters close to its Alameda home. By May l984 the 'Big E' and CVW-11 were ready for another 7th Fleet cruise, the carrier embarking its air wing at the dockside prior to setting sail. VF-114's last WestPac aboard the *Enterprise* ended on 16 March 1990, the squadron (and the rest of CVW-11) then transferring its allegiance to the brand new *Nimitz* class carrier USS *Abraham Lincoln* (CVN-72) *(US Navy photo)*

Right Celebrating 20 years of service with the Tomcat in October 1992, VF-124 'Gunfighters' have trained thousands of F-14 pilots, RIOs and maintenance personnel for frontline fleet squadrons over the past two decades. Equipped with a mixed fleet of Alpha, Bravo and Delta model F-14s, VF-124 is tasked with turning nugget aircrew fresh from training squadrons in Texas and Florida into fully proficient naval aviators ready for fleet service. Utilizing a tried and tested syllabus which covers all aspects of the Tomcat from how its powerplant works to basic ACM, the 30 fully-qualified flying instructors at VF-124 run an intensive prograrmme which usually lasts between six and eight months. For many years VF-124 have only decorated their F-14s with the traditional 'NJ' training wing codes. However, in 1987 the squadron resprayed two jets in full unit colours in response to a CNO directive which stated that frontline squadrons could decorate a pair of their aircraft in pre-TPS camouflage if they so wished. Prior to taking on the task of training Tomcat crews, VF-124 had spent 14 years as the West Coast 'Crusader College', performing the RAG duties for all the Miramar-based F-8 and RF-8 units *(Angelo Romano)*

As mentioned previously, the US Navy Reserve operates four fully-fledged Tomcat units that are assigned the fighter tasks for CVWR-20 and -30. the Reserve Atlantic Fleet Wing (CVWR-20) utilizes the services of VF-201 'Rangers' and VF-202 'Superheats', both units being based at NAS Dallas. This jet was photographed on an ACM hop over Texas in October 1987, only a matter of months after it had been delivered to VF-201. The unit maintains an active life in support of frontline squadrons, performing an annual training syllabus which closely mirrors the programme undertaken by full-time fleet assets. For example, in March 1991 VF-201 sent five Tomcats to Key West for Dissimilar Air Combat Training (DACT) with VF-45 'Blackbirds'; the following month the unit completed a MissilEx at Naval Station Roosevelt Roads, Puerto Rico, which included firing one Phoenix, five Sparrow and three Sidewinder missiles; carquals were carried out aboard the USS *Dwight D Eisenhower* (CVN-69) in May; the 'Rangers' deployed to Fallon in October to support CVW-5's pre-cruise work-ups, and then took part in exercise *Pecos Thunder* with the USAF and ANG at Holloman AFB; and in November VF-201 headed west once again to Miramar for another MissilEx *(US Navy Reserve photo)*

VF-202 'Superheats' usually accompany VF-201 on many of these deployments as the squadrons strive to maintain a close working relationship and an element of commonality in operational procedures. Both reserve units at Dallas received very early Block 60/65 Tomcats that had spent most of their service lives in storage. Accruing only a handful of hours in manufacturer's check flights, the aircraft were mothballed in 1976/77 as later block airframes with increased capabilities were by that stage available to the fleet. Finally retrieved from storage in early 1986, the F-14s were shipped to Grumman's Calverton plant and totally rebuilt (new wiring, plumbing and full spec avionics were fitted) to bring the aircraft up to Block 135 standards. This jet was photographed during a CVWR-20 det to NAS Fallon in August 1988 *(Michael Grove)*